PRAISE FOR *PAUL ON IDENTITY*

"A probing, provocative reading that captures Paul's affinities with ancient Stoic philosophy while also exploring the nuances of his Jewish self-understanding as redefined by a distinctive form of 'Christ faith'—all this viewed through the interpretive lens of identity, both ancient and modern. A thoughtful contribution to the current debate about identity politics."

—Carl R. Holladay, Charles Howard Candler Professor Emeritus of New Testament, Candler School of Theology, Emory University

"Can Paul speak today to a world that does not share his original theological framework? In this bold and engaging book, Troels Engberg-Pedersen answers 'yes,' offering an original analysis of Paul's two-level notion of identity that resolves an impasse in Pauline studies and at the same time offers resources to address the identity dilemmas of the modern West. Clear, accessible, and provocative, this is a timely book that invites and deserves a wide readership."

—John M. G. Barclay, Lightfoot Professor of Divinity, Durham University

"Not since Rudolf Bultmann, and never with such historical seriousness, has anyone so brilliantly realized the task of translating Paul's thought into a message for moderns, and with a focus on contemporary issues of identity."

—Stanley Stowers, professor emeritus, Brown University

"All serious New Testament scholars have a distinctive vision of Paul that is grounded in years of intense study. That is certainly the case for Troels Enberg-Pedersen, who shares with us here his understanding of the apostle in a form that is simultaneously lucid, accessible, and provocative. It is vintage Troels."

—John T. Fitzgerald, professor of New Testament, Notre Dame

"Those who know Troels Engberg-Pedersen's work will recognize the immense learning and his trademark rigor. But this is also a gripping read as well as going far beyond what most biblical scholars would attempt. It is illuminating and challenging, presenting not only a Pauline theology but nothing less than a manifesto for Western democracy."

—Simon Gathercole, professor of New Testament, University of Cambridge

PAUL ON IDENTITY

PAUL ON IDENTITY

THEOLOGY AS POLITICS

Troels Engberg-Pedersen

Fortress Press
Minneapolis

PAUL ON IDENTITY
Theology as Politics

The author considers all Scripture translations to be his own due to incorporated changes and added emphasis throughout.

Cover image: Giotto (1267–1337), *Saint Paul*, Basilica Papale di San Francesco, Assisi
Cover design: Savanah Landerholm

Print ISBN: 978-1-5064-7404-5
eBook ISBN: 978-1-5064-7405-2

In memoriam

Heikki Räisänen

CONTENTS

PREFACE

WRITING THIS BOOK has been a labor of love. As I explain in the introduction, I wanted to write a book on Paul for both experts and non-experts that is based on my own contributions to scholarship but is also more accessible and wide-ranging. That was both a challenge and a joy. In the book, I also wanted to quote liberally from the Pauline letters themselves in order to let the reader understand and savor the incredible richness of Paul's writing. That has been a joy too. Finally, I wanted to focus on a topic that is very much with us at present: that of identity in all its complexity. Thinking about that topic has been fascinating.

This book was published in an earlier version in Danish in 2020 by Gyldendal Publishers, Copenhagen. I am grateful for positive reactions to that version from, among others, my longtime, esteemed colleague in Copenhagen Mogens Müller and my splendid Norwegian New Testament colleagues Halvor Moxnes and Karl Olav Sandnes. Since then, I have rewritten it extensively in English for an American public. During that period, I was engaged in a long, fruitful discussion, published by the online forum Syndicate, with Paula Fredriksen (Boston and Jerusalem) of her recent, important book *Paul: The Pagans' Apostle* (2017). That discussion has left its mark on chapter 3 of the present book, for which I am grateful. I also thank here my scholarly friends Dale B. Martin (Yale) and Margaret M. Mitchell (Chicago) for most valuable help on the American version, in particular the conclusion, where they raised many pertinent questions. Finally, I am very grateful to the executive editor of Fortress Press, Dr. Carey C. Newman, for having accepted to publish the book in what has long been a very distinguished press in Pauline matters and also for his and his team's unstinted, professional help in its production. It is, I believe, to the great credit of Fortress Press to be willing to publish a scholarly book on Paul that also addresses a wider public.

I dedicate the book to the memory of the master of New Testament studies in Finland, Heikki Räisänen (1941–2015). In his many books, not least *Paul and the Law* (1983), *Beyond New Testament Theology* (1990), and his magisterial *The Rise of Christian Beliefs* (2010), Räisänen developed a comparative religions approach to the New Testament texts that was intended to give all the material studied its own due. A Festschrift for Räisänen (2001) was appropriately entitled *Fair Play*. Räisänen was internationally recognized as one of the best representatives of a critical, open-minded, and liberal tradition in Nordic scholarship on the New Testament. In Pauline studies, this tradition also counts such earlier distinguished scholars as Danish Johannes Munck (1904–65), Norwegian Nils Alstrup Dahl (1911–2001, who went to Yale), and Swedish Krister Stendahl (1921–2008, who went to Harvard). Though not myself a close friend of Räisänen, I invited him to Denmark to discuss Paul, met him several times at conferences in Finland, and always enjoyed both his sharp intellect and his characteristically Finnish kindness.

INTRODUCTION

AIM AND OVERALL PROFILE

HISTORY IS WHAT has made us who we are. But history is also more than that. It contains a huge number of ideas and practices that human beings have adopted in order to handle the challenges of life and from which we may ourselves learn. In both respects, our own history is therefore more than just interesting. Do we not want to know who we are and how we have come to be who we are? And do we not want to become better at seeing our own possibilities in handling the challenges of life by coming to see how others have done it?

This is why there is every reason to publish a book for non-specialists and specialists alike on a figure of central historical importance in our Western culture: the apostle Paul. Paul, to a very high degree, fulfills the two dimensions of the importance of history that I mentioned. He has played a central role in making us (Westerners) who we are. And his thought contains ideas that—quite independently of their specifically Christian framework—offer solutions to problems with which we are ourselves also confronted in our current situation.

In writing here also for non-specialists, I am attempting to address a general academic readership with something like the *Volksbuch* (a "people's book") on Paul published in 1907 by a scholarly hero of mine, the German William Wrede (1859–1906). (Hence the avoidance of footnotes in this book.) So much has happened in scholarship since then, and our current political situation is of course entirely different. But Wrede's splendid attempt to be both scholarly and much more broadly accessible remains a model. With such an intended readership, however, the book has not been written specifically for non-specialists who—without necessarily having any deeper knowledge of Paul—will in principle expect to agree with him. In other words, I am not specifically addressing Christians. Instead, my intended audience is anybody who is interested in understanding the historical Paul so well on his own premises that one can also see what use one may make of him in the cultural and political situation in the West of the 2020s.

However, the book is *also* meant for specialists on Paul. In spite of its accessible character, it is not just a summary of what I have hitherto published on the apostle. Instead, I am attempting in my usual philosophical fashion to bring it all together and to develop the inner connections of Paul's views on so many different issues into a single comprehensive view. For this purpose, I introduce and show the pervasiveness and usefulness of the notion of a "double model" of identity in Paul, which has not been offered elsewhere. I also attempt to show the intimate connection between the core set of ideas in Paul and his rhetorical practice, again in a manner I have not seen elsewhere.

Paul has had a huge importance in Western culture, which even today is largely defined by Christianity. He has been called "the second founder of Christianity," and this is not totally off the mark. Remember that Paul's letters constitute the oldest literary remains we possess from early Christianity. They were written around the middle of the first century CE (perhaps between 49 and 54), and the gospel narratives about Jesus in the New Testament (under the names of Mark, Matthew, Luke, and John) are all later: from shortly after 70 CE onward. So Paul was there first. And not just that: his influence has been colossal. For somebody who has the least degree of historical consciousness and curiosity, Paul must be a godsend—if not literally so, then certainly in the metaphorical sense. What did he want to say? Why is he so important?

However, that is not my only reason for writing this book. I also follow in the footsteps of a number of modern philosophers who have discussed Paul within the last two to three decades as a way of thinking about current political problems in our modern world. Three of the most important are these: German Jacob Taubes (1923–87) and two who are still living, Italian Giorgio Agamben (born 1942) and Frenchman Alain Badiou (born 1937). Badiou's book from 1997, *Saint Paul: La fondation de l'universalisme* (*Saint Paul: The Foundation of Universalism*), is particularly relevant for my own concerns. Is Badiou right that Paul "founded universalism"? What, in any case, is universalism? And how may we use it in the current political situation?

Another immediate source for my own concerns is a book from 2018 by the American political scientist Francis Fukuyama, *Identity: Contemporary Identity Politics and the Struggle for Recognition*. How should we understand the concept of "identity" that plays such a huge role in modern Western culture? How should we handle the phenomenon of "identity politics," which according to Fukuyama has come to stay—with all the problems that it raises? And not least this: How—if that is at all possible—should we combine identity politics with a postulated universalism? In short, how do we want to understand ourselves and to relate to one another? Fukuyama's book does not mention Paul, but it is focused on a basic problem that is found already in Paul—indeed, one that he addresses intensely: the relationship between what is shared by us all (in Paul, all Christ believers) and what is distinctive of each individual (or group of individuals) among us.

It goes without saying that reading Paul with such questions in mind is reading him very much from the outside. We are who we are as a result of a long historical development. We cannot just throw all of that overboard when we are reading an author who lived two thousand years ago. What it was possible for him to think and believe is not necessarily possible to think and believe for us. If we then also read Paul in the light of modern problems of identity and universalism, which are concepts that were not distinctly articulated in that way by Paul himself, then we are clearly reading him from the outside.

Nevertheless, it is a fascinating aspect of all this that we also need to read him from the inside, as best we can. We must try to understand what *his* world looked like and what *he* wanted to say into that world. This is something we can do by engaging energetically in historical work, which builds upon the imagination—that is, our capacity to imagine how the world may have been hanging together for a person who apparently looked at it in *this* way and in *that* way (as we can see from what he says). Of course, it is we ourselves who are engaged in that reconstruction. We can never get completely away from ourselves. But we *are* capable of getting much closer to the past than if we just read Paul as our contemporary.

This is also something we *need* to do. Otherwise, we will not be able to find out what *he*, Paul, may be able to tell us about the questions we ourselves pose. Initially, we therefore need to give Paul the benefit of the doubt. What is it that *he* wanted to say? What did his world look like? And what did he want to say to certain other human beings (the addressees of his letters) *within* that world? It is only once we have answered these questions that we may go on to ask what light Paul may throw on our own questions.

I said that I have not written this book specifically for Christians. In spite of that, it follows from what I have just said that my curious and open-minded readers must acknowledge the presence of ideas in Paul that they might not accept on their own—but with which many Christians will in one or another way agree. This holds, for instance, for a set of ideas that are absolutely central to Paul: after his death on the cross (here we might all agree), Jesus, who is also Christ (the Messiah), was resurrected from the dead and raised into heaven; here he was sitting at the right hand of God, the Father, and from there, he would again come to appear (in the air and very soon) to judge the living and the dead, some of whom would be lost forever while others would be saved to the same kind of resurrection and eternal life in heaven. Most of this is already stated in the oldest Christian text that we possess—namely, Paul's first letter to the Christ believers in Thessaloniki (1 Thess 4:15–17):

> **Text 0.1 (T0.1)** 15For this we declare to you by the word of the Lord [i.e., Jesus], that we who are alive, who are left until the coming of the Lord, will by no means precede those who have (already) died. 16For the Lord himself, with a cry of command, with the archangel's call and with the sound of God's trumpet, will descend from heaven, and the dead in Christ will rise first. 17Then we who are alive, who are left, will be caught up in the clouds together with them to meet the Lord in the air; and so we will be with the Lord forever.

Modern Christians confess all of this in the Christian creed, including those Christians (like myself) who cannot believe it in the literal sense in which it was surely meant by Paul. However, when we wish to *understand* Paul, we all have to imagine that it was true. Otherwise, we just do not grasp what he is saying. At this point of the present book, therefore, anybody who is not prepared to give Paul this amount of the benefit of the doubt is welcome to close it!

If we therefore have to follow Paul himself a considerable part of the way in order to understand him at all in his own historical context, won't the whole exercise be boring? Not at all! Paul was without doubt a genius. By developing the meaning of the Christ faith in the many ways he did, he alone created a basis for living that was both new and all-inclusive in the sense that it, as it were, covered the whole world and was also *addressed* to the whole world. To follow this and see how it unfolds is in itself fascinating. But

Paul was also a living individual whom we may follow in a large number of versions in the letters he wrote to the congregations of Christ believers that he had founded. Paul is directly—and I mean directly in his language—present for us across a distance of more than two thousand years. That is one reason I quote so much from him throughout this book. By means of these quotations, the reader will get a strong impression of Paul himself. Also, it is my hope that by grappling with these quotations, the reader will gradually come to understand Paul much better. Superficially, Paul is not easy. However, once one has become accustomed to his way of writing, he becomes much easier to follow. And the gains are enormous. The translations from the Greek are basically taken from the excellent New Revised Standard Version, but they are to be considered my own, since I have very often made changes where I felt it was needed, either in substance or for the purpose of emphasis. Throughout, the aim has been to make Paul come alive to the modern reader as clearly as possible. A genius deserves to be experienced directly. That is also the reason why I have identified all the quoted Pauline main texts in this book with a tag (**T0.1**, **T0.2**, etc.). In this way, the reader is enjoined to look back or forward to the relevant text and read it in its new contexts. My intention has been to create of web of Pauline texts in the book itself so that the reader may gradually come to fully experience Paul's writerly genius. You don't need to look it up in the Bible: read it here!

Thus the reader of this book is invited to undertake a historical journey that shows what Paul's agenda was, what opposition he encountered, with what means (of rhetoric and ideas) he attempted to disarm the opposition, and finally, who this rather unique person was. In addition, we will see that precisely within his own historical context, Paul managed to develop some ideas that are also directly relevant to us today in our current political situation.

Later in this introduction, we will consider the structure of the book in slightly more detail. Before that, we need to remind ourselves of certain facts about Paul's letters and about the apostle himself. We will stay with what is minimally necessary, but even here, experts will see that I am making decisions on issues that might be endlessly discussed. Where the issues are both central and more controversial, I will note it.

SOME FACTS ABOUT THE LETTERS

The genuine Pauline letters. The New Testament contains thirteen letters that have traditionally been seen as part of the Pauline collection of letters (the *Corpus Paulinum*). Most scholars (and I agree) consider only seven of these to be genuine in the sense that they go directly back to the apostle Paul himself. The remaining letters derive from some kind of Pauline "school" consisting of authors who wanted to speak in Paul's name. (We *know* very little about such a "school.") I list the genuine letters here in what is at least one likely chronological order: First Thessalonians, Galatians, First Corinthians, Philippians, Philemon, Second Corinthians, and Romans.

The recipients and the genre and character of the letters. As is clear from their titles, the letters are named (in the tradition but not by Paul himself) after their recipients. With an original basis in the important city of Antioch in Syria, Paul had engaged in two missionary journeys, first in Asia Minor (now Turkey) and next in Greece. The letters were written after the second journey to the small congregations of Christ believers that Paul had founded in various cities during these travels. For instance, there were congregations in Thessaloniki and Philippi in northern Greece and in Corinth in central Greece. Four of the seven genuine letters were written to these. Incidentally, we also know from 1 Thessalonians (3:1) that Paul had stayed in Athens. That is at least worth remembering when one reads Paul's magnificent speech on the Areopagus Hill in Athens given in Acts of the Apostles chapter 17 (17:16–34). (On the Paul of Acts, see later in this introduction.)

Galatians and Philemon differ somewhat. The former was written to a group of congregations founded by Paul on his first missionary journey, probably in the interior of Asia Minor / Turkey (around present Ankara). The latter is addressed, not to a whole congregation, but to a certain individual, Philemon, who also lived in Asia Minor (in the southwestern part).

Romans, which is probably the latest letter, was written in Corinth during Paul's third missionary journey (the second time he visited the congregations he had founded in Greece) in preparation for one more missionary journey that he planned, going from Greece (via Palestine) to Rome and the western Mediterranean (even as far as Spain). Romans differs from the other letters in that it is addressed to Christ believers in Rome whom Paul did not know beforehand. The Roman congregation had not been founded by Paul. In fact, the letter serves as a kind of introduction for Paul himself in preparation for his upcoming visit to the city on his way farther west.

All the letters—and this even includes Romans—serve to address certain *conflicts* that had arisen in the congregations. Paul aims to solve these conflicts in such a way that he might help achieve his ultimate aim for the congregations: unanimity. Even in Romans, he addresses conflicts, of which he must have been told, and argues intensely throughout the letter to solve them and bring about the unanimity that he so strongly desires (Rom 15:5–6—the italics in the Biblical quotations are always mine; italics were not used in antiquity):

> **T0.2** [5]May the God of steadfastness and encouragement grant you to *be of one mind among one another*, in accordance with Christ Jesus, [6]so that *together* you may *with one voice* glorify the God and Father of our Lord Jesus Christ.

Thus the letters are genuine letters, not tractates in letter form. What is more, I consider it likely (we really cannot *know*) that Paul even invented this Christian genre in which he addresses the recipients in an authoritative manner as an "apostle" (i.e., a messenger) of Jesus Christ with encouragement and injunctions. In their overall character, the letters are therefore hortatory. They are, in the language of scholarship and of the theological tradition, "paraenetic"—coming from the Greek *paraínesis*, which means "exhortation" and "encouragement." Thus the letters have a concrete, practical aim: to create agreement, harmony, unanimity. As part of this, however, they are also full of more general reflection on what the world as a whole looks like now that Jesus Christ (the Messiah) has died, been raised, and will very soon return to judge the living and the dead. In his first letter, Paul expresses as follows this overarching framework for the way one should concretely live (1 Thess 1:9–10):

> **T0.3** [9]For the believers of those regions [Macedonia and southern Greece] report about us what kind of welcome we [i.e., Paul and his co-workers] had among you, and how *you turned* to God from idols, *to serve* a living and true God, [10]and *to wait for* his Son from heaven, whom he raised from the dead—Jesus, who rescues us from the wrath that is coming.

The rest of the letter is then concerned with bringing out how the Thessalonian Christ believers should live in the brief interim period in the light of this overarching framework.

What we see here is that there is the closest imaginable connection in Paul between his "theology" (i.e., his ideas about God and Christ and the relationship of human beings to *them* [vertically, as it were]) and his "ethics" (i.e., his ideas about how human beings should live with *one another* [horizontally] in the *light* of the "theology"). While they may be notionally distinguished, as I have just done, "theology" and "ethics" are not separate from one another in Paul and must not be separated. One may mark this by means of scare quotes, speaking of "theology" and "ethics": when Paul wants to solve conflicts in the congregations by means of his letters, the reason is that he aims to create and support the form of life in the congregations ("ethics") that matches and is derived from his "theology." However, since scare quotes are ugly and hamper the reading, I will leave them out in what follows.

The similarities and differences of the letters. In addition to these basic similarities between all the letters, there are a number of differences. *First Thessalonians* (the earliest letter) is a small pearl that shows some of the basic elements in Paul's theology (compare **T0.1** and **T0.3**) and also the intimate connection of these elements with Paul's ethical paraenesis (exhortation). It is also noteworthy that the well-known triad of faith, love, and hope makes its appearance already here (in that order: 1 Thess 1:3). It is not found so often elsewhere, but it is nevertheless presupposed. And of course it reappears in 1 Corinthians in the famous chapter 13 on love—and here in what has become its "proper" order: faith, hope, and love (1 Cor 13:13). Actually, one might well argue that the order in 1 Thessalonians is better. Faith comes first (in the present), then love (both present and future), and then hope—for the future. Noteworthy is also the fact that the "spirit" (Greek *pneuma*), which plays a central role in later letters, does make an appearance in 1 Thessalonians (e.g., 1:5) but is not developed so extensively as later. However, the pneuma turns up in a strong manner toward the end of the letter as an entity that lives in the Christ believers and in this way contributes to making them holy (1 Thess 5:23):

> **T0.4** 23May the God of peace [as opposed to conflict] himself sanctify you entirely; and may your pneuma and soul and body be kept sound and blameless at the coming of our Lord Jesus Christ.

Here, too, where Paul speaks of the Thessalonian Christ believers' bodies, souls, and pneuma (no matter how this should be understood in more detail), one sees the indissoluble connection between theology and ethics. If the reader who is not already an expert wishes to read something by Paul himself that is both relatively short and not too difficult—but also quite striking—then 1 Thessalonians is the best place to go.

The next letter among those that are easier to understand is probably *Philippians*. (Many scholars consider this to be Paul's last letter, even after Romans. I disagree.) This, too, is relatively short, and here—like in 1 Thessalonians—Paul presupposes that the congregation is not torn by divisions. (When that happens, the letters invariably become more complex.) Paul is in jail (which I take to be in Ephesus in western Turkey), from where he sends the letter to Philippi in northern Greece as a letter of thanks for a financial gift he has received. The tone of the letter is therefore quite forthcoming, even warm. But Paul would not be Paul if he did not employ the occasion to exhort the Philippian Christ believers to "live your life in a manner worthy of the gospel of Christ" (Phil 1:27). And he would not be Paul if he did not justify this, first, by giving a more expanded account of the underlying theology—that is, his ideas about what God has done through Jesus Christ—and second, by telling them what this has all meant to himself. The first thing happens, for instance, in a famous so-called hymn (which is hardly a hymn but rather a piece of high prose) that tells of the coming on earth of Jesus Christ and his return to heaven (Phil 2:6–11). The second thing happens, for instance, in Paul's introductory account of the circumstances around his being in jail (1:12–26) and in a very personal and compact account of his own experience of the death and resurrection of Jesus Christ (3:4–16). Philippians is much richer than 1 Thessalonians and introduces Paul himself much more strongly than there. But it remains relatively easy to understand.

The very short, personal letter to *Philemon* stands somewhat apart. As we noted, it addresses a single individual, Philemon, asking him to take back in the proper Christian manner one of his slaves, Onesimus, who had run away. It is a good question, to which we will come back, whether Paul is even asking Philemon to *manumit* poor Onesimus. At least, he does not say so explicitly.

The four remaining genuine letters fall into two groups. First and Second Corinthians were written on two different occasions to the congregation in Corinth. In *First Corinthians*, which is a long and incredibly multifaceted letter, Paul addresses a range of specific issues raised directly by the Corinthian congregation in a letter to Paul or made known to him in roundabout ways. Do they have sex outside of marriage? Do they take mutual grievances to court before the "unrighteous" (i.e., non-believers) and not before the "saints"? Do they *not* wish to have sex, not even in marriage? How about eating meat that may have been sacrificed to pagan gods? When women pray or speak prophetically at service, should they wear a head covering? How should the poor and the rich celebrate the Eucharist together? Indeed, how should the congregation handle a situation during service in which some people suddenly begin to speak in tongues? All these questions are treated in detail in 1 Corinthians chapters 5–14. But the discussion is framed by the theology of the letter, which Paul gives in chapters 1–4 and 15 (the latter on the resurrection of Christ believers), and by some concluding exhortations and greetings in chapter 16. There are good reasons 1 Corinthians has become the central letter when scholars have attempted to analyze the social life of a Pauline congregation both within the congregation and in relationship to the outside society. It is a formidable letter.

Second Corinthians is totally different. Here the tone has become almost desperate and much harsher. It is desperate because Paul feels that the congregation, which he has himself founded, is slipping away through his fingers. It is harsh in its handling of some opponents from the outside (they are "pseudo-apostles" [2 Cor 11:13] and "ministers of Satan" [11:14–15]) who have apparently succeeded in convincing the Corinthians that Paul was "humble when face to face with you, but (only) bold toward you when I am away" (10:1). He adds (10:10),

> **T0.5** [10]For they say, "His letters are weighty and strong, but his bodily presence is weak, and his speech contemptible."

Seen in this light, how should *we* characterize Paul's letters, and here not least 2 Corinthians itself? Is it weighty and strong? The answer should no doubt be yes. At the same time, one must admit that this letter is also so exceedingly complicated in all its power that one is forced to ask whether the poor Corinthians had any chance of understanding what the apostle is saying. Superficially, of course, the message is utterly clear: Follow me! Do what I say! But the justification that Paul gives and the whole manner in which he brings himself into his picture of the overarching theology are so complicated and de facto deep that one can easily understand two things. First, it is probable (though we do not *know* this) that some of the Corinthians turned their backs on Paul. Second, many modern scholars have given up trying to understand the letter as a unity, taking it instead to consist of three, four, or even five letter "fragments" that have been more or less haphazardly stitched together to form the present canonical letter. This hallowed idea is—by my lights—wrong. But it does require a somewhat imaginative reader to follow the apostle's wild line of thought in this letter. Precisely for that reason, however, 2 Corinthians is perhaps the letter that leads one most deeply into the unique symbiosis of Paul's overall agenda and his own person—through a magnificent rhetorical display. We will look more closely into this in chapter 6.

What remains are Galatians and Romans, which are tied together by their theme: the relationship between Christ faith and the rest of Judaism. Of these two letters, it is the shorter and earlier letter to the *Galatians* that makes Paul's case most clearly.

Should the Galatians, who were non-Jews who had become Christ believers when Paul was previously with them, let themselves be circumcised (for the men), thus becoming "real" Jews who also followed the law of Moses? This was demanded (or at least suggested) by some Christ-believing preachers who had turned up in the congregations after Paul had left them. Paul, however, argues strongly that the answer is no. Christ faith is fully sufficient for the kind of salvation that all are seeking. The converted Galatians must not submit to the law of Moses and become Jews by letting themselves be circumcised. On the contrary, "I wish that those who are unsettling you [by arguing for circumcision] would cut the whole thing off" (Gal 5:12), as the apostle humbly says. And he adds (6:12–15),

> **T0.6** 12It is those who want to make a good showing in the flesh that
> try to compel you to be circumcised—only that they may not be
> persecuted for the cross of Christ. 13Even the circumcised [or those
> who preach circumcision] do not themselves obey the law, but they
> want you to be circumcised so that they may boast about your flesh.
> 14I, by contrast, may I never boast of anything except the cross of
> our Lord Jesus Christ, by which the world has been crucified to me,
> and I to the world. 15For neither circumcision nor uncircumcision
> is anything; but a new creation is everything!

And Paul plays his trump card (6:17–18):

> **T0.7** 17From now on, let no one make trouble for me; for I carry
> the marks of Jesus branded on my body. 18May the grace of our
> Lord Jesus Christ be with your pneuma, brothers. Amen.

Nobody knows what those marks looked like. But the Galatians are at least told that in Paul, they could, as it were, see the crucified Jesus Christ himself (compare earlier in the letter: Gal 3:1–5 and 4:12–20—**T6.2** and **T6.3** in chapter 6). Paul was not exactly modest.

Galatians is a complex letter that has played a huge role in the history of Christianity and continues to be controversial, not least with regard to the question of (the Jewish) Paul's relationship with (the rest of) Judaism. It is also a truly fascinating letter in a number of respects. For one thing, we can see here how important philosophical ways of thinking and arguing became for Paul as he reflected on the non-Jewish Galatians' relationship with the Jewish law. Here we may note a huge development from the relatively unphilosophical 1 Thessalonians. It is as if the new question forced Paul to think more philosophically about his message. For another—like in 2 Corinthians, where Paul is also up against the wall—in Galatians, too, one gets a strong sense of Paul "himself" (or as we will see in chapter 6, his *persona*: the self-image that he constructs) as he confronts his opponents behind and among the Galatians.

Finally, there is *Romans*, in which Paul provides a presentation of himself to the Romans by summarizing the whole of his gospel, once again focusing on the relationship between Christ faith and the rest of Judaism. It is noteworthy that in this summary, he recapitulates central parts of Galatians (not least in Rom 5–8) and a whole set of arguments from 1 Corinthians (not least in Rom 14–15). Romans is a genuine letter and not the theological tractate—or even Paul's theological testament—that earlier scholars have found in it. But it is also apparent that in giving a presentation of himself in Romans, Paul is attempting to bring the different motifs from his earlier letters together in something like a unified account of his theology and ethics. (Even here, though, it is likely that Paul continues to respond somewhat more ad hoc to what he takes to be misinterpretations of his position among the Romans.) In the light of this overall character of the letter, one must speak of a development from the five easy chapters of 1 Thessalonians to the sixteen incredibly rich and complex chapters of Romans that is nothing if not striking. It is almost like the development in Beethoven from his first to his ninth symphony! Now it is certainly the case that Paul has delivered a letter that is both weighty and strong. Moreover, the development in philosophical sophistication that we already noticed in connection with Galatians now reaches its culmination.

Is this development also one of content? Does Paul understand his own message differently in different letters? That might of course be the case. Nevertheless, as already noted, there are many central ideas that remain in place throughout. One is the expectation of the imminent return from heaven of Jesus Christ to judge the living and the dead. We saw this already in 1 Thessalonians (4:15–17, **T0.1**). And we see exactly the same in Romans (13:11–14):

> **T0.8** [11]Besides this, you know what time it is, how it is now the moment for you to wake from sleep. For salvation is nearer to us now than when we became believers; [12]the night is far gone, the day is near. Let us then lay aside the works of darkness and put on the armor of light; [13]let us live honorably as in the day, not in reveling and drunkenness, not in debauchery and licentiousness, not in quarreling and jealousy. [14]Instead, put on the Lord Jesus Christ, and make no provision for the flesh, to gratify its desires.

Just as the imminent return of Christ was a given, so are all the other basic elements in Paul's thought. One must certainly speak of a strong development in the way Paul *expands* on his understanding and gives it philosophical sophistication and legitimation. But I do not believe that we see any real changes in its basic content.

Paul in the letters and in later texts of the New Testament. As noted above, the seven genuine letters were perhaps written between 49 and 54 CE. (This, however, is highly controversial.) In addition, the New Testament contains six letters by "Paul" (Ephesians, Colossians, 2 Thessalonians, 1-2 Timothy, Titus). They all belong to the

Pauline "school" we mentioned and have taken up motifs from the genuine Paul and continued them in the various directions the writers felt a need for. The four gospels, which in the canon are printed before the Pauline literature (but which are all *later* than Paul), do not deal with Paul but go back to the beginning of the movement by narrating the story (in varying forms) of Jesus Christ. It is different with the Acts of the Apostles, which was probably written by the evangelist Luke sometime after 100 CE. Initially, the main character here is Paul's colleague Peter, but gradually, Paul becomes the central character—once Luke's Peter has behaved in the proper "Pauline" way, for instance, by extending the message of Jesus Christ to non-Jews (Acts 10). (Luke was very much concerned with showing the unanimity within the early church, not least among its peers.) It is interesting to note that Acts ends at precisely the point in history to which Paul's own genuine letter to the Romans also points: his arrival in Rome. That is probably also part of the reason Acts has been placed where it belongs in the New Testament: after the four gospels—but just before Romans.

The description of Paul given in Acts has had enormous influence on the image of Paul in posterity, not least the thrice-repeated account of his so-called conversion to Christ faith in chapters 9 (Acts 9:1–19), 22 (Acts 22:3–21), and 26 (Acts 26:9–20). In spite of this, it is necessary to insist that the whole account given in Acts reflects interests and perspectives of its author (Luke), who was working more than fifty years after Paul, and not directly those of the historical Paul. For him, we must basically build on the genuine letters alone. Fortunately, that is also enough for our purposes.

WHO WAS PAUL?

If we build on the seven genuine letters, there is admittedly not that much that we can say about the historical Paul. But there is something. First, he was a Jew who belonged to the sect within Judaism called Pharisaism, which consisted of especially pious Jews with their own, somewhat more rigid understanding of the law of Moses. That he himself was a Pharisee is clear from an intense passage in Philippians in which he described his own call to the Christ faith (Phil 3:2–11). This is such a powerful passage that we need to quote it in full. Paul begins by warning the Philippians against other preachers of the Christ gospel who have a more directly Jewish agenda than Paul's own:

> **T0.9** [2]Beware of the dogs, beware of the evil workers, beware of those who mutilate the flesh! [3]For it is we who are the circumcision, who worship (God) in the pneuma of God and boast in Christ Jesus and have no confidence in the flesh—[4]even though I, too, have reason for confidence in the flesh. If anyone else has reason to be confident in the flesh, I have more: [5]circumcised on the eighth day, a member of the people of Israel, of the tribe of Benjamin, a Hebrew born of Hebrews; as to the law, a Pharisee; [6]as to zeal, a persecutor of the church; as to righteousness under the law, blameless. [7]Yet whatever gains I had, these I have come to regard as loss because of Christ. [8]More than that, I regard everything as loss because of the surpassing value of knowing Christ Jesus my Lord. For his sake I have suffered the loss of all things, and I regard them as rubbish, in order that I may gain Christ [9]and be found in him, not having a righteousness of my own that comes from the law, but one that comes through faith in Christ, the righteousness from God based on faith, [10]in order that I may know Christ and the power of his resurrection and the sharing of his sufferings by becoming like him in his death, [11]*if* somehow I may attain the resurrection from the dead.

Nobody should come and declare themselves to be a better Jew than Paul! And so he is happy to list the various features of which he might himself boast if he were to engage in that kind of comparison. However, that would precisely be wrong (from 3:7 onward). Instead, it is all now *only* a matter of Christ faith, of knowledge of Christ, and of "finding oneself in" Christ. The latter takes two forms: both in the present, when Paul takes the shape of Christ in his death and shares with him in his sufferings, and also hopefully in the future, when he will himself reach the resurrection from the dead that corresponds to the one that Christ has already achieved. This is all both magnificent and difficult to understand. What is Paul in fact talking about? We will come back to this. Here the point lies in the earlier part of the passage: that Paul was a Jew who was in all respects as good as any other—something that he in a way continued to be. (And please remember that the idea of Christ was itself a Jewish one throughout.)

What does he mean when he says that before his call, he had been a persecutor of the "church"? We know the answer from the account of Paul's call in Acts chapter 9. Fortunately, we also know it from another intense description by Paul himself in Galatians chapter 1 (1:11–17):

> **T0.10** [11]For I want you to know, brothers, that the gospel that was
> proclaimed by me is not of human origin; [12]for I did not receive it
> from a human source, nor was I taught it, but I received it through a
> revelation of Jesus Christ. [13]You have heard, no doubt, of my earlier
> life in Judaism. I was violently persecuting the church of God and was
> trying to destroy it. [14]I advanced in Judaism beyond many among my
> people of the same age, for I was far more zealous for the traditions
> of my ancestors. [15]But when God, who had set me apart before I was
> born and called me through his grace, was pleased [16]to reveal his Son
> to me, so that I might proclaim him among the Gentiles, I did not
> confer with any human being, [17]nor did I go up to Jerusalem to those
> who were already apostles before me, but I went away at once into
> Arabia, and afterwards I returned to Damascus.

Here Paul describes a call of the kind one knows from similar calls of prophets in the Jewish Bible. They are charged by God to do this or the other thing. Paul's task was to preach the gospel of Jesus Christ among non-Jews, those whom Greek-speaking Jews called *ta ethnê*, the gentiles or all who were not Jews. This task was entirely opposed to everything Paul had previously taken to be mandatory. As a good Pharisee who was filled with religious zeal (something one would probably—viewed from the outside—call fanaticism), he had previously thought that one should attempt to destroy the new Jewish sect of people who took Jesus (of Nazareth) to be the Jewish Messiah (Christ). By contrast (and as he says, "through a revelation of Jesus Christ"), he now recognized the central claim of the sect—*that* Jesus was the Messiah / Christ—and received the further task of preaching this to non-Jews. *How* Jesus Christ was revealed to him is something we are not told.

It is worth noting, however, that Paul elsewhere describes his call in a manner that resembles the one given in Acts by speaking of something that has to do with light. Since we seem to be here at the heart of Paul's own experience of his call, I give the relevant text (2 Cor 4:5–6):

> **T0.11** [5]For we do not proclaim ourselves (to you); we proclaim Jesus Christ as Lord and ourselves as your slaves for Jesus' sake. [6]For it is the God who said, "Let light shine out of darkness," who has *shone in our hearts to give the light* of the knowledge of the glory of God *in the face of Jesus Christ.*

Just as God created the light at the creation of the world (Gen 1:3: "Then God said: 'Let there be light'; and there was light"), so God also let a light shine in Paul's heart so that he was "enlightened" and received knowledge of God's glory as reflected in the face of Jesus Christ. Note here that Paul is no doubt referring to a vision: he *saw* (with his inner eye) God's *glory* (probably a form of shining, that is, something visible—in fact, God's "*spirit*") in the *face* of Jesus Christ (again something visible). But note too that the vision is also a cognitive one as pertaining to some form of knowledge.

Back in Galatians, how did Paul receive from God (or Christ?) the task of preaching the new message specifically to non-Jews? He may not himself have known. Perhaps he basically got an *idea*—namely, that what had now been revealed to him (Jesus was and is the Messiah / Christ) had a meaning that made it equally relevant to non-Jews and to Jews. A little further on in Galatians (2:1–10), he at least tells of a meeting in Jerusalem at which the missionary field was divided between the apostles: Peter would take care of the Jews and Paul of the non-Jews.

There is an important point here. In spite of the fact that Paul has in **T0.10** described his earlier life as having been "in Judaism" (Gal 1:13), we should not take it as if the new faith in Jesus Christ was suddenly something that no longer belonged within Judaism. Paul was and remained a Jew. And his Christ faith was Jewish. The fact that he now saw it as relevant not just to Jews but also to non-Jews does not change any of this. What it does do is raise a very precise question: How should Jews and non-Jews relate to one another now that they have both confessed to faith in Jesus Christ? Should the Christ-believing non-Jews become Jews? If not, what are they? And conversely, should the Christ-believing Jews no longer be Jews? In that case, what are *they*? With this set of questions, we have arrived at the central theme of this book concerning identity.

First, however, we must conclude on what we know about Paul. He was a Pharisee and a good Jew. What more do we know about his life before he was called as an apostle of Jesus Christ? Not much, but on the basis of the letters themselves, we *can* say something. He had received a good education. It is likely (though in fact not mentioned in the letters) that he came from the Greek city of Tarsus on the Mediterranean coast of southeastern Asia Minor / Turkey, not so far from where the coastal line goes south and Syria begins. From the letters themselves, we can see that his mother tongue was Greek. He read his Jewish Bible (what in the Christian tradition became "the Old Testament") in the Greek version of the so-called Septuagint. At school (a Greek-speaking gymnasium?), he must have learned to write in Greek in a manner that is not only correct but also incredibly alive. In Tarsus, there also was a tradition of Greek philosophy, which included one of the major philosophical schools, Stoicism (on which more later). From the letters, we can see that Paul did have some knowledge of motifs and ways of thinking of Greek philosophy, both Stoicism and Platonism (on which again more later). Thus Paul was himself an exponent of a culture that was mixed, both Jewish and Greek. But seen from his own identity perspective, it was Judaism that was central. Paul was and remained a ("Hellenized") Jew.

What we find here is an interesting duality. On the one hand, human beings may in their whole way of life and thought reflect cultural impulses that are in fact derived from different original cultures. They run together in people even though their origins are different. On the other hand, the same people may see themselves in terms of their identity as specifically belonging to one of the original cultures. Paul saw himself not as a Greek (or, for that matter, a Roman, even though he may have had Roman citizenship) but as a Jew—and now also as a Christ-believing one.

In addition to having a certain education and an identity as a Jew, Paul was also what I mentioned before: a genius. We have perhaps stopped using that term (but wasn't Einstein a genius?). However, it has been used of Paul by one of the greatest living experts on Paul, the American E. P. Sanders, in connection with a question that has plagued scholarship: Is Paul always consistent? Does everything he says in the letters hang fully together in the last resort? Sanders answered no—and that is why Paul is a genius! A genius tries out ideas without being concerned about consistency. The rest of us then try to make it all fit together. In that sense, Paul was a genius—even though there may well be considerably more consistency in Paul than Sanders allowed.

Thus far we have spoken of Paul's life before and up to his call and his missionary journeys. How did he end his life? We know from Romans that once he had "proclaimed the good news of Christ from Jerusalem as far round as Illyricum [i.e., modern Albania]" (Rom 15:19), Paul had planned two things. He would first go back to Jerusalem with a gift of money to the holy ones there (15:25), a gift that he had collected in his congregations in Greece (15:26–27). Next, when the gift had been delivered, he would turn round and travel the whole way to Spain and "visit you on the way" (15:28–29; see also 15:23–24). It was in order to prepare for this visit that he wrote Romans.

The rest is silence if we go by the seven genuine letters alone. By contrast, the last third (chapters 21–28) of the Acts of the Apostles is full of stories about the apostle's fate: he was arrested in Jerusalem, appealed his case to the emperor in Rome, and was therefore transported to the capital, where he arrived in the last chapter of the work. Here he was allowed to live by himself, with a soldier to guard him (Acts 28:16), and he did so for as many as two years, during which he "welcomed all who came to him" (28:30). The last thing we hear is this (28:31):

> **T0.12** 31[He was] proclaiming the kingdom of God and teaching about the Lord Jesus Christ with all boldness and without hindrance.

Tradition has it that in the end, Paul was executed in Rome. Acts does not say so, but the whole account in chapters 21–28 of the way Paul was seized and brought before various Roman and Jewish authorities is so heavily colored by the account given of Jesus's death in the gospels that one must take it that the result was the same. Paul was executed just as his Lord, Jesus Christ, had been. Let him, then, have the last word as stated in the letter to the Philippians that he wrote from an earlier prison (Phil 1:21–24):

> **T0.13** [21]For to me, living is Christ and dying is gain. [22]If I am to live in the flesh, that means fruitful labor for me; and I do not know which I prefer. [23]I am hard constrained on either side: my desire is to depart and be with Christ, for that is far better; [24]but to remain in the flesh is more necessary for you.

Paul was wholly ready to die in order to be together with Christ. And he literally meant it.

THE STRUCTURE OF THE BOOK

These remarks about the letters already give us the structure of the book: the agenda, the opposition, and the persuasion, including the person. In chapters 1–2, we will examine Paul's basic agenda. Here the topic is Paul's theology (chapter 1) and ethics (chapter 2) and not least the intimate connection between the two. Here, too, we will meet a number of central ideas that people living in the twenty-first century cannot make their own in the form in which Paul understood them. But as I have urged, we must take Paul at his word. Once that has happened, we will also consider some questions that we may ourselves have and make an attempt at a certain actualization. Are there any ideas in Paul that we may use in some form or other, even though it will probably not be precisely in Paul's own way? We will begin to address this question in these two chapters.

In chapters 3–4, we will investigate the opposition that Paul encountered and his ways of handling them. Here we primarily meet three conflicts that are all about identity: between Jews and non-Jews, between masters and slaves, and between men and women. Paul himself identifies these three topics as the central ones when he says the following in Galatians (3:26–28):

> **T0.14** [26]For in Christ Jesus you are all sons of God through faith. [27]As many of you as were baptized into Christ have clothed yourselves with Christ. [28]There is *no longer Jew or Greek*, there is *no longer slave or free*, there is *no longer male and female*; for *all of you are one in Christ Jesus*.

Exactly what does this mean? For instance, "male" and "female" hardly disappears. And we have already seen that the difference between Jew and Greek was not *meant* to disappear: the non-Jews must precisely not let themselves be circumcised and thus be turned into Jews. In what way, then, "is" there neither Jew nor Greek in Jesus Christ? How does Paul's postulated universalism—or at least his basic idea of a complete unity and community in Christ—relate to those differences of identity that continue to be there? Are we already here able to see some Pauline idea that is relevant to the relationship between universalism and identity politics?

In addition to these three central pairs of conflicts, Paul also treats a number of conflicts in his letters that touch on other sides of the human being. The topic of sexual ethics contains three issues (homosexual practice, divorce, sexual renunciation) that Paul discusses in ways that also explain why these types of questions remain central in modern religions. We on our side must examine how his solutions relate to his basic idea of community in Christ. The same holds of another central theme, which concerns the relations of Christ believers to the world around them. Were believers allowed to participate in dinners with non-believers at which meat might be served that had formed part of sacrifices to pagan gods? Were Christ believers meant to pay taxes to non-Christ-believing authorities? Could they take cases to pagan courts? We will see that Paul constantly attempts to handle these concrete issues in relation to his central idea. Once we have done that, we will also ask whether there is something in this that we may ourselves employ. In many cases, the answer will be no. In other cases, the answer may be different.

We have already seen that the Pauline letters are basically hortatory. They aim to bring something about in their addressees. In chapters 5–6, we will examine the rhetorical means by which Paul aimed to generate persuasion in his addressees. He does this by appealing partly to inclusion (of all members of the congregation with one another and with himself; chapter 5) and partly to exclusion (of opponents coming from the outside; chapter 6). We will see that he makes use of some recurring patterns of persuasion. One of them, which is quite central, is his use of himself. Paul is himself very strongly present in the letters. He constantly appeals to his earlier contacts with the addressees. He also often recounts what has happened in the period between his first visit with them and the moment when he is writing the letter. And he strongly appeals to the addressees by using himself as an example of how they, on their side, should be. All the time, it is Paul, Paul, Paul—and then also them! This general use of Paul himself in his relation to the addressees certainly serves the function of persuasion. But it can (and should) also be understood as an expression of the core idea itself: Paul is even attempting to *create* the community between himself and his addressees that constitutes the core idea. But not just that. Paul is never just happy to apply his own authority to his addressees. He also lets his core idea of a real community fall back on himself in order to give room for the identity of *the others*. The very way in which he handles his persuasion itself reflects the connection he has seen between what is shared and universal, on the one hand, and the identity perspective of the individual, on the other. Is there anything in this that we, on our side, may also use? We must consider that. At least, it is difficult to reject the idea that the content of any given message must also be relevant to the way in which it is presented.

In chapter 6, we will examine Paul's persuasion when he argues for exclusion of external opponents. Here we will also address the theme of Paul's person. What is meant by this is not the so-called historical Paul, as it were behind the letters, but rather the Paul who comes to expression in the letters themselves, what I will call Paul's *persona*. There is no doubt that this is a constructed Paul: Paul as he appears through his account of himself. But that is not a problem. On the contrary, we here have something manifest (in the letters themselves) that we may try to understand directly. The reason we will also focus on Paul's *persona* is that he appears so manifestly in the letters themselves with a certain identity. How does this individual identity relate to the shared identity that is his overall topic? Is there room for Paul's own identity within the community for which he is arguing? Is the community capable of containing an apostle who is also a genius? By asking in this way, we may hopefully get to the core of our guiding question concerning the relationship between universalism and identity politics.

From the agenda via the opposition to the persuasion and the person: in one way, it is the two first themes that are central. They are what the letters are most directly about, their literal content. In another way, it is perhaps the two last themes that are central. This is where it all becomes concrete and real. Here a human being is acting in ways that we are able to see directly. In addition, this is where one can see the intimate connection of the overarching ideas with the social practice of an individual person.

In the conclusion, we will first summarize our findings and then compare Paul's ideas with the modern discussions of national identity and identity politics given by the American political scientists Francis Fukuyama and Deborah Schildkraut. Here we will see that Paul does have something important to say also for our current political situation. It will also become clear that one can only see this once one has grasped what Paul himself says in all its coherent complexity as we have analyzed this in the preceding chapters. That accounts for the structure of the book. One has to go through so much that is fascinating in itself but also basically historical before one can see its high relevance to us now.

1

PAUL'S AGENDA

THE NEW CREATION

IN THIS CHAPTER, we will look at the foundational part of Paul's central concerns, which is his view of what God had done to human beings when he sent Jesus Christ down on earth. The theme here is specifically Paul's "theology": about God, Christ, and the (vertical) relationship of human beings to them. In the next chapter, we will look at Paul's "ethics": the (horizontal) relationship of human beings to one another as seen in the light of the theology.

A NEW CREATION THROUGH DYING TO THE FLESHLY WORLD

In Galatians, Paul articulates his central concern in the following way, which we already know from the introduction (**T0.6**, Gal 6:12, 14–15):

> (**T0.6**) [12]those who want to make a good showing in the flesh. . . . [14]I on my side: may I never boast of anything—except the cross of our Lord Jesus Christ, by which the world has been crucified to me, and I to the world. [15]For neither circumcision nor uncircumcision means anything; but *a new creation* does.

In this text, Paul introduces a radical dualism. On the one side, we have the "flesh" and the world at large. On the other side, we have Jesus's cross—and Paul, who makes a confession to that. In this construction, the cross stands for a total rejection of the flesh and the world (Paul has been "crucified" to them), and that makes sense. If the death of Jesus Christ on a cross is meant to be all that matters, something to which one is wholly directed, then one's own body and in general the whole ordinary world become completely indifferent. But why on earth should anybody make a confession to Jesus's death on the cross? Paul's answer in this passage is that in *Jesus's* case, "the cross" stands, not just for his death, but also *through that means* for something altogether new and positive: a new *creation*, which includes the idea of a new *life*. How so? Answer: God created something wholly new when he let Jesus die and *be raised* again from the dead to a new life. Admittedly, Jesus's resurrection is not explicitly mentioned here, but it is elsewhere, as we will see. *That* is what turned Jesus's death into a new creation. (By contrast, a sheer death on a cross is *not* a new creation!) The same thing then also holds for Paul himself when he makes a confession to this combination of Jesus's death on the cross and his resurrection. For him, too, there is something altogether new and positive: a wholly new creation, a new life.

We will consider as we go along a number of aspects of how Paul understands this radical dualism. Here let us note what he means by the flesh and the world. When he speaks in the present context of the flesh, he is almost making a joke. His opponents want to make a good showing in the flesh, he says. They concretely aim to perform circumcision on the poor Galatian men (and then, says Paul, to boast about it to their Jewish compatriots). Circumcision, of course, takes place in the flesh—in fact, in a very sensitive piece of flesh. In this way, the "flesh" (Greek *sarx*) stands directly for the body. But in Paul, sarx also stands for *everything* that happens in our ordinary, earthly world and is focused on our bodies. For instance, the kind of recognition that Paul's opponents aim to acquire from their compatriots is a social relationship. In Paul, this too falls under sarx. We will later consider what his rationale was for this. Basically, the idea is that the human *body* carries a certain *self-awareness*, which implies a certain self-*directedness*, and that this self-awareness and self-directedness are also involved in a phenomenon like social recognition. Thus Paul's idea of the sarx is at the same time both very concrete and narrowly focused on the body itself—and also much broader, though still with a basis in the body. In fact, as he himself says in the present passage, the sarx covers the whole world, to be understood as everything that takes place in our world with a basis and starting point in our bodies: everything that is *not* seen to be connected with Jesus's death and resurrection.

Against sarx stands, in Paul's world, the "spirit" (Greek *pneuma*). The radical dualism that he articulates in the passage is also one between sarx and pneuma. Paul speaks extensively of the pneuma earlier in the letter, as we will see later, but he leaves it out here. The most likely reason is that he now wishes to balance two things in his confession. There is Jesus's death on the cross, which means that the rest of the world also dies (for Paul, that is), and there is also something entirely new: a completely new creation. Later, we will see that the pneuma is in fact an *instrument* for this new creation: it helps bring it about. Right here, however, what is in focus for Paul is the idea itself of a wholly new creation through Jesus's *death*, a creation that through that means has turned its back completely on the bodily world.

Thus what is expressed in the passage is a movement in a person (here Paul himself) *from* the ("sarkic," earthly) world that is based on the body and its concomitant self-awareness and self-directedness *via* an exclusive mental focus on Jesus's death on the cross (and his resurrection), which makes one turn one's back on the bodily world, *to* a completely new creation—and hence a new life. We must evidently develop further what this new creation actually consists in. In a way, that is what the rest is all about, both in Paul himself and in this book.

Since we are here specifically interested in Paul's understanding of identity, it is worth quoting from an important text earlier in the letter, to which we will come back in chapter 3. The text belongs at the end of chapter 2 of Galatians, but as soon as one attempts to grasp the overall structure of the letter, one will see that it points directly forward to the passage at the end of the letter that we have just considered. In the text from chapter 2, Paul describes his own identity in a striking manner that he will then precisely take up in **T0.6** and generalize to the idea of a new creation. Paul says this of himself (Gal 2:19–20, see in **T3.3**):

> (**T3.3**) 19I, by contrast [i.e., Paul himself as opposed to his colleague Peter] have *died* to the law through the law, so that I might *live* to God. I have been *crucified with* Christ; 20and *it is no longer I who live,* but *it is Christ who lives in me.* To the extent that I now live in the flesh, I live in faith, faith in the Son of God, who loved me and gave himself for me.

A few verses earlier, Paul describes how he and Peter came to realize that "righteousness" (Greek *dikaiosynê*, normally translated as "justice"), which is the proper relationship with God, could come about not through following the law of Moses but only through Christ faith (2:16). (We will consider the meaning of this in detail later.) In 2:19–20, he then applies this specifically to himself and begins to speak of being "dead" to something and "alive" to something else. The language is striking: Paul has been "crucified" together with Christ and himself "no longer" lives. What is expressed in these ways is Paul's conception of his own identity, of who he himself is. He is one who is defined by one thing alone: faithfulness (Greek *pistis*) in relation to Christ and specifically to Christ's death on his own behalf. Paul *is* nothing other than this. All the other things one might mention (compare "to the extent that I now live in the flesh") are wholly irrelevant to this identity. It is this change of identity away from attaching any significance whatsoever to the fleshly values of the world that Paul brings out by means of his metaphorical statements that he has been "crucified" together with Christ and "no longer" lives. At the end of the letter, then—in **T0.6**—he makes it explicit that being crucified *with* Christ is also being crucified *to* the whole world—and that this means an altogether new creation, a wholly new life.

The movement that we noted in **T0.6** (*from* the world *via* Jesus's death *to* a new creation) is found in another striking passage: 2 Corinthians 5:14–17.

> **T1.1** [14]For the love of Christ constrains us, because we have concluded that one has died for all—*therefore* all have died. [15]And he died for all, so that those who live [in spite of the fact that they, too, are dead—namely, to the world] *might live no longer for themselves, but for him who died and was raised for them.* [16]From now on, therefore, we know no one according to the flesh. Even though we may have known Christ according to the flesh, we know him no longer in that way. [17]So if anyone is in Christ, there is *a new creation*: everything old has passed away; see, something new has been generated!

"Everything old has passed away": Paul was genuinely a revolutionary. For he actually meant it. In this text, we again meet the idea of a focus on Jesus's death on the cross, which means that one is, in one's self-understanding, dead to anything else in the world. One may of course continue to live, but even then, one lives no longer—as Paul explicitly says—for oneself but only for Christ, who both died and (here Paul is wholly explicit about it) was resurrected for one's own sake. From 5:16 onward, the text spells out how such a life should be understood. One no longer "knows" anybody according to the flesh—that is, one no longer attaches any importance whatsoever to any person's bodily based, self-aware, and self-directed ("sarkic") character. The same is true even of Christ, as Paul dares claim in an outburst that verges on hubris. Not even him does one "know" according to the flesh. Of course, Christ (in the shape of Jesus) was by now physically dead. But here Paul is almost saying that even if the earthly Jesus had been alive, one would not have "known" him so as to attach any importance to him. He would have been completely indifferent in comparison with all the radical things that have in fact already happened: if somebody is "in" Christ—that is, in the *risen* Christ—then there is a wholly new creation, then one *only* "knows" the risen Christ. It is difficult to find a stronger way of expressing Paul's radical dualism: to die with Christ in such a manner that one no longer lives for oneself but lives in a wholly new creation only for the risen Christ.

In what way may one be "in" Christ? We will consider that in a moment. Some scholars have spoken of a "Christ mysticism" here. That, however, is just as mystical as what it is intended to elucidate. In addition, it is, to my mind, false. As we will see, there is nothing mystical about Paul's idea. Instead, it is wholly concrete.

The perspicacious reader may have noted that in the two quoted passages from Galatians (**T0.6** and **T3.3**), Paul focuses on Jesus's death but does not speak so clearly about his resurrection and the new life that this implies. That only happens in the passage from 2 Corinthians (**T1.1**). The reason is purely contextual and rhetorical. In the Galatians passages, Paul aims to emphasize what one dies away *from* in being directed toward Jesus's death (and resurrection). In the Corinthians passage, by contrast, he aims to bring out what one comes to live *for* in being directed toward both Jesus's death and his resurrection. Paul no doubt had both sides in mind in all three passages (after all, in **T3.3**, he speaks of "*living* to God"). He just handles the conglomerate of death and resurrection differently depending on his contextual agenda.

So far, we know that Paul operated with a radical dualism between the world based in bodies with individual self-awareness and self-directedness and the new creation (including that of human beings) that God had brought about through the death on the cross and resurrection of Jesus Christ. We need to have this central understanding in place before we can go on to ask exactly how it relates to all those other identities (of being Jews or non-Jews, masters or slaves, men or women, etc.) that continue to be present in the bodily based world of human beings. For even if Christ believers do die to these identities so as not to attach any importance whatsoever to them, they will continue to live as individual human beings without having left them completely behind. Those other identities will continue to be there. We will come back later (from chapter 3 onward) to the question of the relationship between these two types of identity.

THE FUNCTION OF THE PNEUMA IN THE FUTURE

When and how can we speak of a new creation of Christ-believing human beings? With regard to when, the answer—as so often in Paul—is a double one: both now (in Christ faith) and in the future (at the resurrection on the day of judgment). Paul speaks extensively about the latter in a number of places, and since he is clearest when he speaks of the future, we must begin there.

First Corinthians chapter 15 discusses how one should understand the new human being at the resurrection. Some among the Corinthians have apparently claimed this: "There is no resurrection from the dead" (1 Cor 15:12). Paul replies, But then, neither has Christ risen (15:13) with all the consequences of this (15:14–19). But he *has* risen! Look here (15:20–24, 26, 28):

> **T1.2** [20]But in fact Christ has been raised from the dead, the first fruits of those who have died. [21]For since death came (into the world) through a human being [namely, Adam; see Rom 5:12–21], the resurrection of the dead has also (come into the world) through a human being [namely, Jesus Christ]; [22]for as all die in Adam, so all will be made alive in Christ. [23]But each in his own order:

> Christ the first fruits, then at his coming [i.e., his return] those who belong to Christ. [24]Then comes the end, when he hands over the kingdom to God the Father, after he has destroyed every ruler and every authority and power. . . . [26]The last enemy to be destroyed is death. . . . [28]When all things are subjected to him [Christ], then the Son himself will also be subjected to the one [God] who put all things in subjection under him [Christ], so that God may be all in all.

This is all grandiose. It is also wholly mythic (but not mystical!). It belongs under the way of thinking that we, from a modern perspective, must characterize as "myth." However, for Paul himself, it was the literal truth. This is how it would happen—and very soon. A little later in the chapter, he recounts it all again in the same mythic language (15:50–55, 57):

> **T1.3** [50]What I am saying, brothers, is this: flesh and blood cannot inherit the kingdom of God, nor does the perishable inherit the imperishable. [51]Listen, I tell you a mystery! We will not all die, but we will all be changed, [52]in a moment, in the twinkling of an eye, at the last (day's) trumpet. For the trumpet will sound, and the dead will be raised imperishable, and we will be changed. [53]For this perishable body must put on imperishability, and this mortal body must put on immortality. [54]When this perishable body puts on imperishability, and this mortal body puts on immortality, then the saying that is written will be fulfilled:
>
> > "Death has been swallowed up in victory."
> > [55]"Where, O death, is your victory?
> > Where, O death, is your sting?"
>
> . . . [57]But thanks be to God, who gives us the victory through our Lord Jesus Christ.

This text has made an enormous impression throughout all time. Think, for instance, of Handel's *Messiah* or Brahms's *A German Requiem*, where it is directly quoted. But note also that Paul has in no way lost his philosophical mind. When he says that flesh and blood cannot inherit the kingdom of God, he is relying on the immediately preceding section, to which we will come back in a moment, and the point is that it is not the body of flesh and blood that will be resurrected. Later Christians have changed this when they have insisted on a bodily resurrection. Paul thought differently. Note also that Paul sticks to the idea we already met in the introduction from 1 Thessalonians 4:16–17 (see in **T0.1**) of a precise sequence in the resurrection of human beings. The first to be resurrected will be those who have already died, then those who remain alive will be *changed*, and so on. Note, finally, the intense, almost ritualistic repetitions in 1 Corinthians 15:53–54: it is *this* (perishable and mortal) body that will be changed. (How? See in a moment.)

However, Paul would not be Paul if he did not also want to say something more than to celebrate a "mystery" (1 Cor 15:51) in strongly mythic language. In between the two texts we have quoted from the chapter, he addresses the issue in a much more specific and philosophical manner (15:35):

> **T1.4** [35]But someone will ask, "*How* are the dead raised? With what *kind* of body do they come?"

This fair question is then answered in a careful account (1 Cor 15:36–47) in which Paul first shows that it makes good sense that the body must die before it is resurrected (like a bare seed that will grow up only later) and next goes into more detail on the relationship between the human body of flesh and blood and the body that will be resurrected. We will focus on the latter part only (15:42–49):

T1.5 [42]So it is with the resurrection of the dead. What is sown is perishable, what is raised is imperishable. [43]It is sown in dishonor, it is raised in glory. It is sown in weakness, it is raised in power. [44]It is sown a psychic body, it is raised a pneumatic body. If there is a psychic body, there is also a pneumatic body. [45]Thus it is written, "The first man, Adam, became a living being"; the last Adam became a life-giving pneuma. [46]But it is not the pneumatic that is first, but the psychic, and then the pneumatic. [47]The first man was from the earth, a man of dust; the second man is from heaven. [48]As was the man of dust, so are those who are of the dust; and as is the man of heaven, so are those who are of heaven. [49]Just as we have borne the image of the man of dust, we will also bear the image of the man of heaven.

In this account, Paul is obviously drawing on his Jewish heritage when he speaks of Adam as the first human being and opposes him to "the last Adam," who is Christ. As we noted, this is a contrast that he will reuse in Romans 5 (5:12–21). The contrast evidently suits the idea of a new creation that we already know. To Adam (the first creation) corresponds Christ (the new creation). However, in this text the apostle is also drawing on certain Greek cosmological ideas to be found, in particular, in Stoicism, which he may have gotten to know in his hometown, Tarsus. Stoicism was a philosophical school that had been articulated around 300 BCE by Zeno of Citium (on Cyprus, not so far away from Tarsus) as a kind of successor to Socrates (d. 399 BCE), Plato (427–347 BCE), and Aristotle (384–322 BCE) and that had gathered strength during the centuries that led up to Paul. What is at issue in the passage is the contrast between a "psychic body" and a "pneumatic body." The psychic body is the one we know, a body of flesh and blood. It is a *living* body, since it contains a "soul" (Greek *psychê*). This is already said in Genesis, from which Paul quotes. And it fits closely with what, for instance, Aristotle says in his treatise *On the Soul* (*De anima*): it is the soul that makes a living body living. The pneumatic body, however, is different. Here it is Stoicism, in particular, that offers material for an understanding.

In Stoicism, the world as a whole is kept together by and permeated with "spirit"—that is, pneuma. This is a physical stuff that perhaps consists of a combination of fire and air in an especially fine alloy. This pneuma has its home in heaven, which is understood wholly concretely as a place "up there." Here we find the so-called heavenly bodies, of which Paul, too, speaks in the passage (1 Cor 15:40–41): the sun, moon, and stars. But the Stoic pneuma is also capable of penetrating *everything* in the world, including human bodies. And that is what Paul imagines will happen in an especially striking manner. At the resurrection, the human bodies of flesh and blood will be *changed into* pneumatic bodies of the same kind as the heavenly bodies. Should we then also imagine the resurrected Christ believers on the day of judgment as, for instance, stars? Precisely! Here is what Paul says to the Philippians in a quite different context (Phil 2:14–16):

> **T1.6** [14]Do all things without murmuring and arguing, [15]so that you may be blameless and innocent, children of God without blemish in the midst of a crooked and perverse generation, *in which you shine like stars in the world* [16]while holding fast to the word of life—so that I can boast on the day of Christ that I did not run in vain or labor in vain.

That is how the Philippians should be now: *like* stars. After the resurrection on the day of Christ, they will apparently be so literally.

Paul's reply to the question of the Corinthians as stated in 1 Corinthians 15:35 (**T1.4** above) is therefore the following: the resurrection of the dead (and the transformation of those who are still living) will come about by means of a pneuma similar to the one in Stoicism when their psychic bodies are transformed into pneumatic bodies. Please note here that this is all to be understood in wholly concrete, material terms. Paul's idea of "spirit" was as different as one can imagine from our current way of understanding the term. (Our understanding is derived from a later Christian understanding of "spirit" as something immaterial. This in turn has its ancient philosophical roots, now not in Stoicism but in Plato.)

It is worth quoting three other splendid texts that draw on the same idea of the transformative role and power of the pneuma in the resurrection. One is in Romans (8:9–11):

> **T1.7** [9]But you are not [namely, any longer] in the flesh (*sarx*); you are in the spirit (*pneuma*), since the pneuma of God dwells in you. (By contrast,) anyone who does not have the pneuma of Christ does not belong to him. [10]But if Christ is in you, your body is dead with respect to sin, whereas the pneuma is life with respect to righteousness. [11]If the pneuma of him [God] who raised Jesus from the dead dwells in you, he [God] who raised Christ from the dead will also give life [in the future] to your mortal bodies through his pneuma that (in)dwells in you [in the present].

Note here how Paul in fact equates God's pneuma, Christ's pneuma, and Christ himself. Note also that these three identical entities may live *within* the mortal bodies of Christ believers already in the present. It is this simple idea that explains Paul's meaning when he speaks of "being *in* Christ." There is no special Christ mysticism in this, just some wholly concrete, physical conceptions. That may be the reason Paul does not shrink from telling the Romans that the pneuma "*in*dwells *in*" them. Will they not understand?

We will return to **T1.7**, which also addresses the presence and function of the pneuma in the bodies of Christ believers here and now.

In the present context, it is the last verse (8:11) that matters. Here Paul unmistakably states that the power by means of which God will raise the mortal human bodies on the day of judgment is the pneuma.

The second splendid text comes from 2 Corinthians (5:1–5):

> **T1.8** [1]For we know that if the earthly tent we live in [i.e., our body] is destroyed, we have a(nother) building from God, a house not made with hands, eternal in the heavens. [2]For (while being) in this tent we groan, longing to be clothed with our heavenly dwelling—[3]if indeed, when we have taken it off we will not be found naked. [4]For while we are still in this tent [i.e., the body], we groan under our burden, because we wish not to be *un*clothed but to be *further* clothed, so that what is mortal may be *swallowed up* by life. [5]He who has prepared us for this very thing is God, who has given us the pneuma as a guarantee.

This text almost speaks for itself in its fascinating mixture of metaphors and concrete ideas. It aims to describe the effect of the pneuma on the human body when Christ believers are "clothed with our heavenly building"—that is, when the pneuma (which comes from God) will transform the human body into a heavenly body that is itself permeated with pneuma. In this way—as Paul says with a clear quotation from 1 Corinthians 15:54 (see in **T1.3**)—what is mortal (i.e., the ordinary human, "psychic" body) will be "swallowed up" by life. Think of how one's world would look if one believed in this in wholly literal terms: one's mortal body will be swallowed up by life when it is transformed into a pneumatic, heavenly body! It is not least this belief that gives Christ believers their identity. One begins to understand why Paul speaks of an altogether new creation.

Let us conclude this string of texts on the role of the pneuma in the resurrection body with a text from Philippians (3:20–21):

> **T1.9** [20]But *our* citizenship is in heaven, and it is from there that we are expecting a Savior, the Lord Jesus Christ. [21]He will *transform the body of our humiliation* so that it may be conformed to *the body of his glory, by* the power [the pneuma] that also enables him to make all things subject to himself.

That is how Paul imagined the ultimate salvation. Only few of us are probably able to accept these ideas. But Paul did, and he understood them quite literally. If one wishes to understand him, one must behave as if one did the same.

THE EFFECT OF THE PNEUMA IN THE PRESENT

We have seen that according to Paul, God's pneuma will be active in the future at the resurrection of Christ believers, when their psychic bodies are transformed into pneumatic bodies. But it is equally important to him that Christ believers have received the pneuma already here and now and that it is *already* at work in their bodies. Thus we move back from the future to the present.

It is clear already in Paul's earliest letter that this is how things are (1 Thess 4:3, 7–8):

> **T1.10** [3]For this is the will of God, your sanctification: that you abstain from fornication. . . . [7]For God did not call us to impurity but in holiness. [8]Therefore, whoever rejects this rejects no human but God, who also gives his holy pneuma to you.

God's pneuma is in itself holy, and it makes Christ believers holy when they receive it. We will gradually come to see more and more of what this means.

How and when do Christ believers receive the pneuma? In **T1.10**, it looks as if it happens continuously. Normally, however, Paul imagines that it happens once for all (which does not, of course, necessarily exclude the other picture)—namely, in baptism, which they experience once they have received Christ faith. Thus, for instance, he says in Galatians (3:14) that God's blessing of Abraham was meant to come to non-Jews "in Christ Jesus so that we might receive the promise of the pneuma [i.e., the pneuma that had been promised] through faith." So first faith, then the pneuma. A little later, he states the same in more detail (Gal 3:26–27; 4:6):

> **T1.11** [3:26]For you are all children of God through faith (and) in Christ Jesus. [27]As many of you as were baptized into Christ have clothed yourselves with Christ [compare "clothed" in **T1.8**]. . . . [4:6]And because you are children [namely, through faith], God has sent the pneuma of his Son into our hearts, crying, "Abba! Father!"

In this text, Paul is operating with two stages. Christ faith—that is, trust in God that Jesus is Christ, God's son, who was resurrected from the dead and so on—turns believers themselves into God's sons. That is then *confirmed* in baptism, where believers receive the pneuma with the consequence that when they get up from the baptism bath, they suddenly begin to speak Aramaic, crying, "Abba! Father!" (Try to imagine it!) Only then will they be fully "clothed in" Christ. Should anybody hear this as a piece of magic, then no wonder. For it must have been understood and have functioned just as concretely as in "real" magic. The only difference is that it presupposes a concrete, physical cosmology: God's pneuma is a physical entity that may penetrate human bodies and hearts.

The importance of baptism in this connection comes out in another key text, this time from Romans 8:14–17, in which Paul takes up and develops the text from Galatians:

> **T1.12** [14]For all who are led by the pneuma of God—*they* are sons of God. [15]For you did not receive a pneuma of slavery to fall back into fear, but you have received a pneuma of adoption, in which we cry,

> "Abba! Father!" [16]It is that very pneuma which bears witness with our pneuma that we are children of God, [17]and if children, then also heirs, heirs of God and joint heirs with Christ—if, in fact, we suffer with him so that we may also be glorified with him.

The pneuma gives full status as sons to Christ believers as they show when getting up from the baptism bath, they cry "Abba! Father!" to God. They possess both the pneuma and the status as sons already in the present, earthly life, where according to Paul, they also *suffer* together with Christ—but only in order to be *glorified* together with him in the resurrection. As he says in Romans 8:18,

> **T1.13** [18]I consider that the sufferings of this present time are not worth comparing with the glory about to be revealed to us.

Thus Christ believers find themselves to be more or less happily stretched out between present and future—less happily because of the present sufferings. Through baptism, they already possess the pneuma, but they will also receive it even more strongly at the resurrection, when their psychic bodies will (finally) be transformed into pneumatic bodies. Having received the pneuma in baptism, they also already have the status as sons. (In fact, according to Galatians, they received that status already through faith; see Gal 3:14 and **T1.11**.) But the same status will become wholly manifest at the resurrection. That is why Paul says the following a little later in the text (Rom 8:23):

> **T1.14** [23]Also we ourselves [just as creation at large], who *have the first fruits* of the pneuma, groan inwardly [due to the present *sufferings*] while we *wait for* [final] adoption, the redemption of our bodies.

We should conclude that through their reception of the pneuma, Christ believers have in fact already been transported to the other side in all relevant respects. Even though they may well suffer from the conditions of the present world, they can be sure that they will also receive the full bodily redemption for which they are longing.

THE PRESENCE OF THE PNEUMA IN THE BODY OF FLESH AND BLOOD

A central question remains: How did Paul imagine the body of flesh and blood that a Christ believer continues to have when it has also received the first fruits of the pneuma and is thus already on its way to being finally swallowed up by it? One might think that Paul would leave this question on one side in a kind of clair-obscure. But he does not. The reason is that by using himself as an example, he aims to show the radical importance already here and now of having received the pneuma and to impress that importance on his addressees. It can be seen—so he thinks—from the way in which the pneuma is already now active in transforming the fleshly body. Paul shows this in a passage in 2 Corinthians in which he describes his own body. Please, stay attuned here. For the apostle does not hold back.

Second Corinthians 4:7 directly continues Paul's description of his own call in 4:5–6 (**T0.11**). The first topic here (4:7–12: section 1) is his experience of the physical presence of the call in his own body. Next (4:13–15: section 2), he claims that this whole description is directly relevant to the Corinthians. Finally (4:16–18: section 3), he connects his own way of life in the present in the light of his physical experience with the idea of the future, complete transformation, which he describes in what immediately follows (5:1–5, **T1.8**). Here comes this striking text (2 Cor 4:7–18):

> **T1.15** [1] [7]But we have this treasure [the experience of the call] in clay jars [his physical body], so that it may be made clear that this extraordinary power [the pneuma] belongs to God and does

> not come from us. [8]We are afflicted in every way, but not crushed; perplexed, but not driven to despair; [9]persecuted, but not forsaken; struck down, but not destroyed–: [10]we always carry in our body the death of Jesus, so that the life of Jesus may also be *made visible* in our body. [11]For while we live, we are always being given up to death for Jesus' sake, so that the life of Jesus may be *made visible in our mortal flesh.* [12]So death is at work in us, but life in *you.* [2] [13]But as we have the same pneuma of faith, as it says in Scripture—"I believed, and so I spoke"—so we also believe, and so we speak, [14]because we know that the one [God] who raised the Lord Jesus will raise us also with Jesus, and will bring us into his presence—together with you. [15]Yes, everything is for your sake, so that grace [coming from God], as it extends to more and more people, may increase thanksgiving [from your side], to the glory of God. [3] [16]So we do not lose heart. *Even though our outer person is wasting away, our inner person is being renewed day by day.* [17]For this slight momentary affliction is preparing us for an eternal weight of glory beyond all measure, [18]as we look not at what can be seen but at what cannot be seen; for what can be seen is temporary, but what cannot be seen is eternal.

In the present context, the important verses are 4:10–11 and 4:16. They clearly show that even while Paul was alive here on earth, his body was occupied by two things, not just one: Jesus's death *and* Jesus's life. The former consists of the afflictions that he experiences in his body of flesh and blood; the latter, of the *appearance* of Jesus's (pneumatic) life (is it some form of "shining"?!) that is caused by the presence of the pneuma in the same body. This appearance is already there to be seen now. The same idea is expressed in 4:16, when Paul speaks of the "inner person" in opposition to the "outer person." For here one must remember that the "inner person" is not something "spiritual" in our sense but instead the body of flesh and blood that is permeated with *Pauline* (i.e., material) pneuma (spirit). Verses 4:14 and 4:18 show that this is all to be understood in the light of the future resurrection, a point that is also made clear in 5:1–5 (**T1.8**). But 4:10–11, in particular, also show with all clarity that what Paul calls Jesus's life is *already* present in Paul's mortal and fleshly body—that is, here and now. For as we have seen earlier in this chapter, the mortal and fleshly body will itself *not* be present at the final resurrection in the future. Thus Paul *must* be talking of the present here.

Is 2 Corinthians 4 (and especially 4:10–11 and 16), then, a single swallow? No, for if we look again at Romans 8:9–11 (**T1.7**), we will see that there, too, Paul was able to say of the fleshly body in the present that it is *dead* in those who have the pneuma in them (including the Christ-believing Romans as a whole), whereas the pneuma that is in them (here and now) is life (8:10). Both things (a dead body and also life) are present in them already here and now. But it is clear that the ultimate transformation of their bodies belongs to the future, as Paul also goes on to say in 8:11.

We should conclude from this and the previous section that the pneuma has a central function for Christ believers, not just with respect to the future, where it will transform their psychic-fleshly bodies into pneumatic ones, but also already here and now. When Christ believers receive the material pneuma in their bodies in baptism, a process is *begun* of a wholly real transformation of their psychic-fleshly bodies, which will eventually be completed at the resurrection. The beginning of this process can be concretely seen in Paul's own body. Generalizing from that, we may also conclude that this process begun by the pneuma is the reason Christ believers are already here and now "in" Christ or "belong" to Christ. It thus has direct consequences for their identity. As they understand themselves, they are—through their reception of the pneuma—essentially and exclusively this: "holy," "in Christ," "Christ people." It is as literally as this that we should understand Paul's idea that through the pneuma, there is a new creation already here and now.

* * *

How may Paul have reached these specific ideas about what was due to happen very soon and what had already happened?

Paul was (as scholarship has it) an *apocalypticist*, and he had taken over this whole way of thinking—*apocalypticism*—from Jesus. Jesus, too, preached that what he called "the kingdom of God" was close at hand. God would intervene directly on earth and create a kingdom where all human misery (existentially in the form of illness and death and socially and politically in the form of oppression) would be removed. The last here on earth would be the first in an earthly kingdom that constitutes a clash with all earthly power.

Paul (and other early Christians) reinterpreted Jesus's ignominious death, which was itself a direct expression of both earthly power and earthly powerlessness, as God's own victory over the earthly powers through Jesus's resurrection. Jesus's resurrection had led him into heaven, where God's kingdom was already realized as a counterpoint to the miserable earthly world. Similarly, Paul took it that the redemption and salvation that was just around the corner for Christ believers would take the form that at their own resurrection, they would experience the kingdom of God *in heaven* (see Phil 3:20–21, **T1.9**), not on earth. In Paul, the pivot around which everything turns is the idea of the resurrection, first of Jesus, then of Christ believers.

The conception of the kingdom of God that lies behind all this has its roots back in Jewish so-called apocalyptic thinking more than two hundred years back. Jesus actualized it in his own way; Paul in his. Both Jesus and Paul were radical apocalypticists. God would erase the misery of the world now (or very soon) and here on earth (or in heaven).

It is an entirely different question how *we* should handle these ideas, which historically, were no doubt understood wholly concretely. That question is addressed by modern systematic theology. We will pass it over here but only insist that we cannot make those ideas our own in the wholly concrete way in which they were historically understood.

2

PAUL'S AGENDA

COMMUNITY IN LOVE AND FREEDOM

WE HAVE SEEN how Paul imagined the effect of the pneuma on the bodies of Christ believers both in the future and the present. This pertains to the specifically theological side of Paul's agenda, which is vertical: what God has done, continues to do, and will do to Christ believers based on the way they themselves respond to the death and resurrection of Jesus Christ. We have also seen that Paul's idea about the effect of the pneuma on Christ believers builds upon specific, concretely cosmological conceptions. For instance, the pneuma is a material entity that at baptism penetrates the bodies of believers.

We should add to this, however, that the pneuma also has a cognitive side to it, one that has to do with understanding. For instance, in a splendid passage in 1 Corinthians (1:18–2:16), Paul speaks of a distinct type of wisdom (Greek *sophia*) that only believers have. Of this, he says that "God has revealed (it) to us through the pneuma" (2:10). Thus the pneuma has both a physical and material side to it and also one that is cognitive. That is not strange. First, exactly the same holds of pneuma in Stoicism, which we have already connected with Paul's own conception of it. Second, Paul's whole agenda is just as much a cognitive one as it is material. These two sides cannot in the end be kept apart. (However, it remains a philosophical question to this day how these two sides of the human being should in the end be related to one another.) Finally, the cognitive character of the pneuma also fits the fact that it follows upon and increases *faith*(fullness). For the latter is almost by definition cognitive. It is about understanding.

So far, so good. All of this together constitutes the theological frame for all the rest. But what does it all mean—including the reception of the pneuma—"*ethically*" with respect to life in the present of Christ believers among *one another*, which includes their own personal relationship with others? That is the question to which we will now turn. It pertains throughout specifically to the cognitive side of the pneuma.

THE EFFECT OF THE PNEUMA IN ETHICS: THE CONTENTS

The question has two sides to it. There is first a question about the actual contents of the ethics. If the pneuma helps make believers holy, and if this fact has direct consequences for their ethical life with one another (see already 1 Thess 4:3–8, **T1.10**), then what does the true ethical life consist in? Second, there is a question of the ethical *power* of the pneuma. If believers have become holy already here and now by receiving the pneuma, then *are* they also holy *ethically*? Do they in fact do what they *should* do? This question is particularly pressing, since Paul's letters are fundamentally hortatory or "paraenetic," as we saw in the introduction. If believers are holy also ethically and hence already do everything they should, then why does Paul also *exhort* them to do so?

Let us first consider the contents of the ethics. A key text, to which we will repeatedly come back, is the following one in Galatians (5:6):

> **T2.1** [6]For in Christ Jesus, neither circumcision nor uncircumcision counts for anything; the only thing that counts is faith working through love.

Note here the intrinsic connection between theology and ethics. Faith(fullness), which is directed toward Christ, belongs under theology, but love (the Pauline *agapê*) is—at least here—directed toward other human beings. It therefore belongs under ethics. If we go by **T2.1**, theology and ethics are inextricably connected. One cannot theologically (i.e., vertically in relation to God and Christ) have genuine Christ faith without also acting ethically (i.e., horizontally in relation to other human beings) with love. Important passages in Romans (1–3 and 7–8) show that Paul took the same relationship to hold negatively. That is, if one has a false relationship with God or Christ, then one also has a false relationship with other human beings. This may be difficult to accept for us moderns. But that is the way it was understood by the apostle.

How, then, should we understand Pauline love? The answer is given a little later in Galatians. Earlier in the letter, Paul has argued that Christ faith means freedom, including from the law of Moses. We will come back to that idea. He continues like this (Gal 5:13–14):

> **T2.2** 13For you were called to freedom, brothers; only do not use your freedom as an opportunity for the flesh, but *through love become slaves to one another.* 14For the whole law [of Moses] is summed up in a single commandment, "You shall love your neighbor as yourself."

This is already helpful. Apparently, love consists in "serving" one another or, in fact, in "being a slave" to one another—that is, to work for the good of *others*. Also, love is not so much a feeling or an emotion as an attitude (toward others) that issues in certain *acts*. Note also that Paul even claims—quite strikingly and actually quite shockingly in light of the way he has been arguing up to then—that this kind of loving is also what is intended by the law (of Moses). Thus in spite of Paul's negative remarks about the Mosaic law earlier in the letter (3:22–23, compare **T2.10**), there is actually no difference here between something called "Judaism" and something called "Christianity." In the end, that is not so strange, since the Christ-believing Paul both was and continued to be a Jew. (Much more on this in the next chapter.)

However, he continues in a manner that both spells out further the character and content of Christ-believing love and shows that in spite of everything, there remains a difference between Christ faith and the Mosaic law. In this context, Paul also explicitly and crucially brings in the pneuma. Here is the whole of this central passage. It shows that Paul was to a very high degree able to think and argue philosophically (Gal 5:16–25):

> **T2.3** [16]What I mean is: live by the pneuma; then you will certainly not gratify the desires of the flesh. [17]For what the flesh desires is opposed to the pneuma, and what the pneuma desires is opposed to the flesh; for these are opposed to each other, to prevent you from doing what you want. [18]But if you are led by the pneuma, you are not subject to the law. [19]Now the works of the flesh are obvious: fornication, impurity, licentiousness, [20]idolatry, sorcery, enmities, strife, jealousy, anger, quarrels, dissensions, factions, [21]envy, drunkenness, carousing, and things like these. I am warning you, as I warned you before: those who do such things will not inherit the kingdom of God. [22]By contrast, the fruit of the pneuma is love, joy, peace, patience, kindness, generosity, faithfulness, [23]gentleness, and self-control. The law is not concerned with such things. [24]And those who belong to Christ Jesus have crucified the flesh with its passions and desires. [25]If we live by the pneuma, let us also walk by the pneuma.

In this passage, Paul philosophically contrasts certain *types of acts* (5:19–21, the "the works of the flesh" of 5:19) with something else, which is a "fruit" of the pneuma and which includes love as the first thing mentioned (5:22–23). The former things are forbidden by the law of Moses; the latter are things that are not treated in the law (see 5:23). The reason, as we should take it, is that they are inner *attitudes*, and no law as a law discusses such things. By contrast, they are precisely a "fruit" of the pneuma that is generated when Christ believers receive it in baptism. It is *these* attitudes that are "active or working (Greek *en-ergeitai*) through love" (see in **T2.1**) in Christ believers—namely, in "works" (Greek *erga*) of love. Thus against a long list of act-types forbidden by the law stands a set of inner attitudes that have been generated by the pneuma and that *issue* in acts of love.

Note also one more crucial difference between the "works of the flesh" and the "fruit" of the pneuma. If we consider carefully Paul's list of the works of the flesh in 5:19–21, we will see that they are all focused either directly on the person's body (fornication, sexual impurity, etc.) or on the individual person in opposition to others (enmity, quarrels, etc.). As we noted in chapter 1, Paul saw an inner connection between focusing on the body and on oneself. Both fall under his concept of sarx. Paul, it seems, was right here. We all *are* our individual bodies. And it makes excellent sense to see a self-directed focus on the individual person as being derived from the self-awareness that goes with being a human body. For instance, when human beings turn other human beings into their enemies, they do it in order to create a social space within which the bodies that they themselves fundamentally are may behave expansively to the detriment of others. Against this stands the fruit of the pneuma, which is all the time directed *positively* toward others—in love (*agapê*), joy, peace, patience, kindness, generosity, faithfulness, gentleness, and self-control (5:22–23). It is in this other-directed sense that Christ believers must "serve one another in love" (see in **T2.2**).

Parts of **T2.3** will occupy us again in discussing the power of the pneuma. So far, the conclusion is that the ethical effect of the pneuma is to reject the type of desire that is based in the body of flesh and blood and in the self-awareness and self-directedness that go with that body. We will see in a moment how radical this rejection is.

We have touched on the relationship between the law of Moses, which forbids the works of the flesh, and the pneuma and its fruit(s), with which the law is not concerned. One more text shows both that the law of Moses (including the Ten Commandments) is highly relevant to the kind of "Christianity" that Paul is articulating (before it existed as being different from Judaism) and also that the law of Moses is in a quite specific way surpassed (but not superseded!) by the Christ faith. The text is from Romans (13:8–10):

> **T2.4** [8]Owe no one anything, except to love one another; for the one who loves another has fulfilled the law. [9]The commandments, "You shall not commit adultery; You shall not murder; You shall not steal; You shall not covet"; and any other commandment, are summed up in this word, "Love your neighbor as yourself." [10]Love does no wrong to a neighbor; therefore, love is the fulfilling of the law.

This is highly compact and full of meaning. When love is *present* (that is the sense of 13:10)—and, as we may add, when it is present as an *attitude* (just as in **T2.3**)—then there is no longer any *use* for the individual commandments contained in the law of Moses. For the person will *already* act in accordance with them. The person who is permeated with the attitude of love and hence will love his neighbor in the Pauline sense will *as a matter of fact* not commit fornication, kill, steal, desire. All these act-types (the works of the flesh) are governed by a focus on the body and the person's self-awareness and self-directedness, both of which are *already* excluded by the attitudes that fall under love. In that sense, Christ faith is Judaism *perfected*.

Another text shows the radical character of Pauline love: Philippians 2:1–4. I quote the whole text, although 2:3–4 in particular is relevant for us here.

> **T2.5** [1]If then there is any encouragement in Christ, any consolation from love, any sharing in the pneuma, any compassion and sympathy, [2]make my joy complete: be of the same mind [namely, as I am], having the same love [namely, for me as I have for you], being in full accord and of one mind [among yourselves]. [3]Do nothing from selfish ambition or conceit, but in humility regard others as better than yourselves. [4]*Let each of you look not to your own interests, but precisely to the interests of others.*

Note how in 2:1–2, Paul appeals to, and even invokes, a sense of community between himself and the Philippians. It is on this basis that he exhorts them in 2:3–4 by drawing a sharp contrast between two attitudes: selfishness and consideration for the good of others. We may speak here of Paul's altruistic "maxim" (like in Immanuel Kant), his fundamental rule of ethics:

> **(T2.5)** [4]*Let each of you look not to your own interests, but precisely to the interests of others.*

Or in our own version, *always* think of the good of others, *never* of your own. It is this very simple (but also wholly radical) idea that constitutes the very content of Pauline love, *agapê*.

So the content of Paul's ethics as generated by reception of the pneuma is love understood in this radical, completely other-directed manner. One might also say that it is community in love. It goes without saying that we must come back to this idea. For no human being *can* live wholly like that. We are all always primarily concerned about ourselves and our bodies. If so, what use may one make of Pauline love?

Before leaving the question of the effect of the pneuma on the contents of ethics, we should note the connection between this theme and our theme in the previous chapter when we spoke of the presence of the material pneuma in the physical bodies of Christ believers. The point is this. In Paul's understanding, the physical body of flesh and blood—the sarx—begins to be conquered by the pneuma when believers receive it in baptism. If, then, the same physical body of flesh and blood—as Paul now rightly contends—is the seat of bodily desire and all those acts that derive from a person's self-awareness and self-directedness, then the physical arrival of the pneuma will have some striking consequences. On the one hand, it will eradicate all those act-types that belong under works of the flesh. On the other hand, it will bring into existence those attitudes like love, joy, peacefulness, and so on that are other-directed and precisely *not* tied to the individual's body, self-awareness, and self-directedness. By its sheer material presence, the pneuma will automatically generate a cognitive change also in the field of ethics.

Note also that when Paul opposes sarx and pneuma in ethics, he retains the radical dualism that we already found in his concept of a wholly new creation. It is this radical dualism that is particularly strongly expressed in the field of ethics in Paul's maxim (Phil 2:4 in **T2.5**):

> (**T2.5**) [4]Let each of you look *not* to your own interests, *but* [precisely!] to the interests of *others*.

We will consider later what to do with this radical stance.

THE EFFECT OF THE PNEUMA IN ETHICS: ITS POWER

First, however, we must discuss the other side of the reception of the pneuma: its power. What Paul has to say about this is once again quite radical—so radical that only a minority among scholars are prepared to accept it. Here it comes out that Paul was what one may call a *faith fanatic*. Christ faith was *necessary* for the kind of salvation that Paul imagined, and we now know what this salvation consisted in: eternal life in heaven. This was due to the fact that Christ faith was further strengthened by reception of the pneuma in baptism, and the pneuma *effected* salvation (in the form of resurrection, etc.). Now, however, there are two further points, one theological and one ethical. The former is that Christ faith—and precisely when it implies reception of the pneuma—was also *sufficient* for salvation. By being in possession of the pneuma, one would also be *certain* of salvation. The other, ethical, point is that as this would hold for the future, so Paul also took it to hold for the present in the way in which the holy person would live among others here on earth. For this person had by now been made completely free of "sin." Such a person was sinless. It is this last point that only a few scholars will accept. What it means is that reception of the pneuma in baptism was *sufficient* to make Christ believers do ethically what they should.

That this is so is already clear from **T2.3** in Galatians (5:16–25). As we saw, Paul here enumerates a list of attitudes that constitute the fruit of the pneuma. These attitudes differ from the act-types that the law forbids (the "works of the flesh") by the fact that the attitudes are *lasting* psychic structures, which will *always* issue in the proper acts. They are in fact what was called "virtues" (Greek *aretai*) in the Greek philosophical tradition—for example, in Aristotle, who defines the virtues as so-called states (Greek *hexeis*). This shows that the power of the pneuma in its fruit (Gal 5:22–23) is complete. When there is the proper *attitude*, then there is no longer any risk of a relapse. Paul immediately confirms this when he declares that "those who belong to Christ Jesus have crucified the flesh with its passions and desires" (5:24). They *have* crucified the flesh—and therefore also its passions and desires! These have in fact been completely eradicated.

However, that is not the way we humans are. So what does the apostle mean? What is more, does he not himself problematize the radical idea of the death of the passions and desires when he states the following in the very next verse: "If we live by the pneuma, *let us* also walk by the pneuma" (5:25)? Of course, the idea that believers "live" by the pneuma might in principle refer to their future resurrection to eternal life. But their "walking" by the pneuma must refer to their ethical life here and now. In that case, is *that* kind of life one to which they need to be *exhorted* (in a kind of mutual summons, "*let us* . . .") if it is also something that they already do? Please, keep that question hanging.

Exactly the same question comes up in connection with another famous text in Romans: 7:7–8:13. This is the text in which Paul declares (by presenting himself as a generalized example of the person who was earlier living under the law of Moses *without* Christ faith) that "I do not do the good that I want, but the evil that I do not want is what I do" (7:15). Let us look a bit more closely at this text. It is strongly disputed but perhaps not quite so unclear as it has been made. Verses 7:5–6 constitute a kind of title for the whole text:

> **T2.6** [5]While we were [nota bene] living in the flesh, our sinful passions, aroused by the law, were at work in our members to bear fruit for death. [6]But now [nota bene] we are discharged from the law, *dead* to that which held us captive, so that we are slaves not under the old written code [namely, the law of Moses] but in the new life of the pneuma.

In this text, Paul contrasts a time *when* (7:5) and a time *now* (7:6). By this means, he divides the text that follows into a much more developed description of the time *when* (7:7–25) and the time *now* (8:1–13). The former time was when one was living (exclusively) under the law of Moses, which while being in itself "holy, just, and good" (7:12)—indeed, even "pneumatic" (7:14)—was also misused by sin, which lives in the human body. Paul spells out the result of this in a hair-raising text (7:14–25). The human being living under the law of Moses (alone), so Paul claims, experienced a deep, inner schism between *wanting* "God's law in my inmost self" (7:22) but also *seeing* "in my members another law at war with the law of my mind, making me captive to the law of sin that dwells in my members" (7:23). This deeply divided person *wills* God's good law but *sees*—that is, must bitterly recognize—that there is another law in the person's body that makes the person do what the law of Moses *forbids*. The schism between wanting one thing and seeing and doing something else is a case of a complete psychic schizophrenia (in Paul's description).

What a relief, then, to get to the description of the time now (8:1–13), when the schism has been overcome! We already know the crucial ideas from 8:9–11 (**T1.7**). Christ believers are no longer in the flesh but in the pneuma (8:9). This means that their bodies are "dead with respect to sin"—that is, actually *dead* (in that respect)! Or more explicitly: they no longer sin; they are completely free of the schism described by Paul in 7:7–25. That is what happened (as Paul has shown a few verses earlier) when Christ came for the first time (8:3–4):

> **T2.7** [3]For what the law, weakened by the flesh, could not do: God sent his own Son in the likeness of sinful flesh, and to deal with sin, and condemned sin in the flesh, [4]*in order that the just requirement of the law might be fulfilled* in us, who walk not according to the flesh but according to the pneuma.

Note here the striking breakdown of the sentence in 8:3, which marks the turn from one thing to the other: from life under the law of Moses alone to life with Christ faith. How did it happen? Well, God sent and so on. Note also the wholly clear account of the purpose of that turn: *in order that* the law of Moses might be *fulfilled* by Christ believers. How, then, *will* it be fulfilled? Through the pneuma. That, and that alone, has the necessary power. That is what Paul describes in 8:9–11 (**T1.7**).

In this way, 7:7–8:11 is one extended argument for the claim that with the arrival of the pneuma in believers, they obtain the power to always and only do what will in fact fulfill the law of Moses. As Paul had already said in Galatians 5:24 (see in **T2.3**), "Those who belong to Christ Jesus have crucified the flesh with its passions and desires." In fact, it makes exquisite sense to see Romans 7:7–8:13 as an extended rewrite of Galatians 5:13–25.

With such an understanding of the relationship between Romans 7:7–25 and 8:1–11, it is all the more striking that Paul ends his whole account of the new state in the following way (8:12–13):

> **T2.8** [12]So then, brothers, we are debtors, not to the flesh, to live according to the flesh—[13]for if you live according to the flesh, you will die; but if by the pneuma you put to death the deeds of the body, you will live.

Apparently, believers are "debtors" to the pneuma. Only if they employ the pneuma to put to death the acts of the body will they themselves live. Why does Paul speak of them as "debtors" (i.e., under an *obligation*) if they already *do* what they should (i.e., if they *already* put the acts of the body to death)? Why does he let his account in 8:1–11 of the way in which believers' bodies are *already* dead (8:10) issue in an (implicit) exhortation that they *should* put their bodies to death?

This question has pestered Pauline research for more than one hundred years. My own answer is that the question derives from a misunderstanding of Paul's "exhortation," his so-called paraenesis. Its aim is not to make Christ believers will and do anything *other* than what they already do. Instead, it aims to *remind* them of what they already both will and do. The exhortation is no more than a reminder. Correspondingly, Paul does not—at least, logically—speak to his addressees in the imperative, telling them what they *should* do. Instead, as we noted in **T2.3** from Galatians (5:25), he engages in a *mutual summons* to make them remember where they already are. A colleague of mine at Aarhus University in Denmark, Professor Kasper Bro Larsen, has thought up a good image to bring the idea across. When Paul exhorts Christ believers, he behaves like their coach in a mental fitness center or gym. They already have strong mental muscles. Now they only need to keep them fit!

We should conclude as follows: Paul's radical idea of the power of the pneuma, which believers had received in baptism, was that this power was so strong that they would already now both want and do what they should in accordance with the law of Moses. In spite of that, however, there might be good reason to *remind* them of this in order to avoid any relapse. When Paul keeps exhorting his addressees in all his letters, he is aiming as their coach—as in a mental fitness center—to strengthen and preserve them in the life that they are already leading. In addition, he probably also aimed to spell out the *particular* content of a life that consisted in having "faith that is working through love" (see in **T2.1**) or in "walking by the pneuma" (see in **T2.3**), for these general descriptions clearly needed to be further specified. But Paul's exhortation does not aim to move his addressees away from where they basically already are. They *have* reached the other side of Paul's fundamental dualism and must now just know and show it in practice.

This point is important for understanding the relationship between life in Christ faith and life under the law of Moses, as Paul understood this according to Romans 7–8. As a good Jew, Paul considered the law of Moses "holy, just, and good" (7:12), even "pneumatic" (in itself, 7:14), and the Jew he is exemplifying in the passage definitely *wanted* to follow it even before he acquired Christ faith. However, that was not always what happened. There remained a gap between the law itself and the Jew exemplified by the pre-Christ-believing Paul, a fissure between wanting to follow the law and wanting something else. This fissure then also takes the form of wanting the *il*licit thing and hence *having* to do what the law prescribes. In this way, the law places people under a real obligation, something they *must* (but do not always) do. Not so in Christ faith. Here believers want one thing and one thing alone—namely, as it happens, what the law of Moses (also) tells them to do. For here the pneumatic law of Moses meets human beings who through Christ faith *have themselves become pneumatic*. When the physical human being of flesh and blood has been completely eradicated, the fissure between wanting and having to do also disappears. Christ believers now want *only* what God's good law (also) tells them to do.

It is this point that Paul brings out when in Romans 8:15 he justifies in the following way his claim that the Romans are God's sons (see in **T1.12**): "For you did not receive a pneuma of slavery to fall back into fear, but you have received a pneuma of adoption, in which we cry, 'Abba! Father!'" Living under the law of Moses (alone) in principle generates fear (in relation to God), since one does not *always* fulfill it, however much one wants to—as Paul has just described in 7:7–25. By contrast, Christ believers have received the pneuma and so always and only do what the law of Moses (also) tells them. Hence they are without fear and no longer live in slavery. They are, as we will see in a moment, *free* by the fact that they by now *only* want what God's good law (also) tells them to do.

We may conclude that Paul's idea of the power of the pneuma in the field of ethics completely matches his idea of the way in which the pneuma, when received in baptism, would (begin to) saturate the physical body of flesh and blood so that he might even say that this body was dead (Rom 8:10, see in **T1.7**). It all hangs together—in its one-sided radicalism.

THE PNEUMA GIVES FREEDOM FROM THE LAW OF MOSES

Paul brings in the concept of freedom in his account of the relationship between living with Christ faith and living only under the law of Moses. In Romans 7–8, he marks the transition from one thing to the other as follows (Rom 8:2):

> **T2.9** [2]For the law of the pneuma of life in Christ Jesus has set you *free* from the law of sin and of death.

The "law" that is mentioned here is in both cases the law of Moses. The difference between speaking of that law as "the law of the pneuma" or "the law of sin" results from two different situations—namely, whether the law of Moses acts on *people* who through Christ faith have become pneumatic or on people who have not. In the latter case, the law generates sin and death, as Paul has just described in 7:7–25. In the former case, the law generates life but also *freedom* from that same law that, because of the person who lives under it alone, became a "law of sin." We may speak here of freedom from the law of Moses taken alone.

Paul had already developed the same idea in Galatians. Here he first describes how "Scripture"—that is, the law of Moses—had "imprisoned all things under the power of sin" (Gal 3:22). He continues (3:23),

> **T2.10** [23]Before faith came, we were imprisoned and guarded under the law until faith would be revealed.

Then the situation became quite different, as the Galatians must not forget (Gal 5:1):

> **T2.11** [1]For *freedom* [namely, from the law of Moses] Christ has set us *free*. Stand firm, therefore, and do not submit again to a yoke of slavery.

However, as we already know from **T2.2** (Gal 5:13),

> (**T2.2**) [13]you were *called to freedom*, brothers; only do not use your freedom as an opportunity for the flesh, but through love become slaves to one another.

Thus the Pauline freedom is, to begin with, a freedom from the law of Moses when the latter is taken on its own, as Jews traditionally did—that is, without any connection with Christ faith. This freedom is brought about by Christ faith and, not least, by receiving the pneuma.

The connection of freedom with the pneuma comes out in another striking passage: 2 Corinthians 3, in which Paul has been concerned once more to contrast Christ faith with the law of Moses taken on its own. As he says, "The letter [i.e., the law of Moses taken on its own without any connection with Christ faith] kills, but the pneuma gives life" (2 Cor 3:6). He ends as follows (2 Cor 3:17–18):

> **T2.12** [17]Now the Lord is the pneuma, and where the pneuma of the Lord is, there is *freedom*. [18]And all of us, with unveiled faces, seeing the glory of the Lord as though reflected in a mirror, are being transformed into the same image from one degree of glory to another; for this comes from the Lord, who is pneuma.

Do we not here meet Paul "the mystic"? Not at all. But one might well celebrate the astonishing, quasi-experiential beauty of a verse like 3:18 in this text. It is precisely both highly imaginative and strictly philosophical. That is the essence of Paul. The idea is that when believers receive the pneuma, they are gradually transformed (compare what we said in chapter 1 about the pneumatic body) into the same "image"—namely, into Christ himself, who is himself pneuma. In this way, they themselves become pneuma. But where Christ's pneuma is, there is also freedom (from the law), as 3:17 has it.

THE PNEUMA ALSO YIELDS FREEDOM FROM THE PASSIONS

To understand this notion of freedom, one must also see that the pneuma yields freedom not only from the law of Moses (taken on its own) but also from the "passions" (desire, greed, and so on; see below), which the law was precisely intended to curb. In fact, it is freedom from the passions as brought about by the pneuma that also *yields* freedom from the law. This inner connection between the passions and the law of Moses is the very theme of Romans 7:5–8:13. That is why Paul may say the following in Romans 7:5–6 (**T2.6** above):

> (**T2.6**) [5]While we were living in the flesh, our *sinful passions, aroused by the law,* were at work in our members to bear fruit for death. [6]But now we are discharged *from the law, dead to that which held us captive . . .*

. . . namely, the law in its connection with the sinful passions. Exactly the same connection is implied in Galatians 5:16–25 (**T2.3** above), where the "works of the flesh" (5:19) are replaced with the fruit of the pneuma (5:22) and where Paul also claims that "if you are led by the pneuma, you are *not subject to the law*" (5:18). We will not discuss here exactly how Paul may have imagined this connection between the law of Moses and sinful passions. It is clear that he did see such a connection. According to Paul, the law of Moses (when taken on its own) *nurses* the very passions and acts that it was also meant to curb. We know from Galatians 5:19–21 (see in **T2.3**) what these passions are: all kinds of desire (Greek *epithymia*; see Gal 5:16; 5:24) that focus on the individual person's body and social status in relation to others. In the same way, Paul brings together everything described in Romans 7:7–25 under the term *desire* (*epithymia*; Rom 7:7), which he understands very broadly. It refers to a wish to obtain everything that individuals want to keep for themselves based on their own body and their individual self-awareness. All of this was (ineffectually) *forbidden* by the law in a manner that led to the miserable situation described in Romans 7:7–25. But this desire was also *eradicated* by the pneuma. And so as soon as Christ believers become free of the passions and actions of the flesh, they will also become free of the law.

We should conclude that Christ faith and reception of the pneuma mean freedom, not just from the law of Moses, but also from the desires and passions that the law was originally intended to curb. Indeed, it is because Christ faith (and reception of the pneuma) generates freedom from the passions that it also generates freedom from the law of Moses (when taken alone)—at the same time, as we know, as it *fulfills* the law.

FREEDOM IN CHRIST

How, then, should we understand this freedom *in* Christ, which is also a freedom *from* the law (taken on its own)? Is it also a freedom to do anything? Of course not, as we immediately see when we recall that freedom from the law is also freedom from the passions. Indeed, Paul himself emphatically answers No! As we know from Romans 7:6 in **T2.6**, the new freedom is a freedom to "serve"—literally, to "be a slave"—in the new life of the pneuma. The content of this is already clear from Galatians 5:13 in **T2.2**, where Paul combines freedom from the law (taken on its own) with the necessity of "serving"—and here, too, literally of "being a slave to"—*one another*. In other words, freedom from the law in Christ also means a freedom to act in accordance with Christ faith, which is precisely "working through *love*" (Gal 5:6, **T2.1**). We already know that this love consists in following Paul's maxim: always think of the good of others, never of your own (see in **T2.5**). Or to put it in the new way, *serve*—or be a slave to—*one* *another*. This element of slavery to others thus is a wholly unproblematic part of the freedom of the Christ believer. By contrast, the other type of slavery, which implies that one does not *wish* to do what one must, is excluded and, indeed, has been *overcome* in Christ faith and reception of the pneuma. In the new situation of freedom from the passions and the law, people who are active through love wish for nothing other than serving and being a slave to one another.

In 1 Corinthians 9, Paul gives a splendid example of this attitude of—as we may call it—*voluntary slavery* to others. In its mixture of precision and constant changes of perspective, it is also a very good example of Paul's genius of language. He first declares (for once, never mind the context) that *as* an apostle and *as* one who has "seen Jesus, our Lord," he is himself free to do what he wishes (1 Cor 9:1). Nevertheless, as he continues a little later (9:19–23),

> **T2.13** [19]though I am free with respect to all, I have *made myself a slave* to all, so that I might win more of them. [20]To the Jews I became as a Jew, in order to win Jews. To those under the law I became as one under the law (though I myself am not under the law) so that I might win those under the law. [21]To those outside the law I became as one outside the law (though I am not free from God's law but am under Christ's law) so that I might win those outside the law. [22]To the weak I became weak, so that I might win the weak. I have become all things to all people, that I might by all means save some. [23]I do it all for the sake of the gospel, so that I may share in its blessings.

Splendid! Here Paul presents himself as an example of the slavery to others that follows from his sense of obligation (the only thing that he himself wills) to the Christ gospel and the freedom that it gives him. *In* that freedom, he has made himself a slave to others.

The Pauline idea of being bound but at the same time also wholly free is reflected in a motif that recurs several times in 1 Corinthians. Apparently, the Corinthians have invoked Paul's own idea of freedom and come to the conclusion that they are free to do whatever they want. All things are permitted (so they claim). Paul immediately agrees: Yes, "*all* things are permitted!" Yet he also immediately adds, "But not all things are beneficial" (e.g., 1 Cor 6:12). In other words, there is freedom in Christ, but not everything is beneficial, neither to the individual nor to the community. And in this context, benefit trumps freedom. What is more, the criterion for whether something is beneficial is quite precise (1 Cor 10:23):

> **T2.14** 23"All things are permitted," but not all things are beneficial. "All things are permitted," but not all things *build up*.

Thus the criterion for whether one is free to act as one wishes is that the *community*—that is, *all*—must be *built up* by what one does, in the wholly concrete sense that *the community is strengthened.* That, of course, is also the direct result of living in accordance with Paul's maxim of always thinking of the good of others and never of oneself. When all are slaves to one another, the community is built up. Thus in Paul, the complete freedom of the individual is intrinsically bound up with a consideration for the well-being of the community. The Pauline freedom is definitely not a freedom to do "what one likes" but a freedom from self-based desires so that one can help others by building up the community. This is a strong idea, to which we will come back.

IDENTITY: THE INDIVIDUAL AND THE COMMUNITY

The idea that "all things are permitted, but not all things are beneficial" has some important consequences for understanding the identity of Christ believers. Who *are* they individually? The answer is this: they are primarily members of "one body in Christ" (Rom 12:5, see in **T2.16**). They may well be different in many respects, but in spite of these differences, they all, together, constitute a single body—which is Christ (and hence the pneuma). Here is one passage in which Paul spells out this idea (1 Cor 12:4–13):

> **T2.15** [4]Now there are varieties of gifts, but the same pneuma;
> [5]and there are varieties of services, but the same Lord; [6]and there
> are varieties of activities, but it is the same God who activates
> all of them in everyone. [7]To each is given the manifestation of
> the pneuma *for the common good.* [8]To one is given through the
> pneuma the utterance of wisdom, and to another the utterance of
> knowledge according to the same pneuma, [9]to another faith by the
> same pneuma, to another gifts of healing by the one pneuma, [10]to
> another the working of miracles, to another prophecy, to another
> the discernment of spirits, to another various kinds of tongues, to
> another the interpretation of tongues. [11]All these are activated by
> one and the same pneuma, which allots to each one individually
> just as the pneuma chooses. [12]For just as the body is one and has
> many members, and all the members of the body, though many,
> are one body, so it is with Christ. [13]For in the one pneuma we were
> all baptized into one body—Jews or Greeks, slaves or free—and we
> were all made to drink of one pneuma.

The last sentence in this text refers to baptism and the Eucharist, respectively. Those are where Christ believers receive the pneuma. And this is self-identically present in all the various gifts in such a manner that all the different persons, who have each their own gift, are together members of the Christ body just as all members of a physical body (which the Christ body of course also is) together constitute a single body. We may parenthetically note that 12:4–6 mentions all three parts of the later Christian so-called Trinity: God,

Christ, and the Holy Spirit. In Paul, however, the point is that all three entities are one. The Lord, too—that is, Christ—and God are pneuma in Paul's world.

In Romans, Paul repeats the idea of a single body with many members but gives it an extra turn (Rom 12:4–5):

> **T2.16** [4]For as in one body we have many members, and not all the members have the same function, [5]so we, who are many, are one body in Christ, and individually we are members one of another.

It is not just that believers are members of the same body. They are also even members of *one another*. So what are they individually? They are defined by the Christ body, to which they individually belong. But they are also defined by *one another*.

Do they not, then, have *any* individuality and identity that is their own? We will consider this question in detail later.

* * *

How was it possible for Paul to believe that Christ believers here and now not only could but also would act in accordance with his maxim—with the result that his constant exhortations were no more than a cheering in the apostle's mental fitness center?

As always in Paul, the answer is double. On the one hand, there is Paul's Jewish apocalyptic heritage (see also the pause reflection, marked by three asterisks, to chapter 1). Paul was a radical apocalypticist. What is more, the gigantic apocalyptic reversal was not just to be expected in the near future (as Jesus had probably thought). It had already begun with the resurrection of Jesus Christ. It is not strange that such an idea might have radical consequences when the apostle wanted to describe what it was that had already happened to Christ believers in the light of Jesus's resurrection—namely, that they had received the pneuma. To conform with the gigantic apocalyptic reversal that had already begun, this event, too, would have radical consequences.

On the other hand, there was what one may well call Paul's Greco-Roman philosophical heritage. In the ethical philosophy of this tradition, which had been founded by Socrates and developed by Plato, Aristotle, and the Stoics, a main concern was to consider how a human being might become morally good (or "virtuous," as they called it). In what way might the specific state of the soul or mind ("virtue") come to be present that meant that a human being would from now on only want and do a single thing, the good? The philosophers gave different answers to this question, but they agreed on the question itself. Similarly with Paul. *Full* goodness, which just as in Aristotle and the Stoics was a matter of attitudes (virtues), would only be present in human beings who had Christ faith. Even more, it *was* present in them! What the philosophers had spoken of as—often quite distant—possibilities, Paul understood as realized. Christ believers had already reached the stage at which others—be it Greco-Roman philosophers or Jewish followers of the law of Moses taken on its own—were only *aiming*. Paul was, in truth, a faith fanatic.

Still, how was it at all possible for Paul to believe that the desires and passions were completely eradicated in pneumatic Christ believers so that they would *only* want one thing (and for that reason always do it)—the good as told by the law?

The answer is that on this point, Paul shared the understanding of one particular philosophical school within the broader field of Greco-Roman philosophy: Stoicism. For the Stoics, happiness, which was the fundamental concern of all the post-Socratic schools, consisted in not having any of the passions—for instance, pleasure, pain, desire, and fear. Happiness consisted in a "lack of passions" (Greek *a-patheia*). Paul took over this idea completely (see Gal 5:24 in **T2.3**). And if one has no passions *whatsoever*, then one will also automatically do the single thing that one both wants to and should do.

Is the result, then, that both the Pauline Christ believers and the Stoic sage have no *emotions* at all? Far from it. On the contrary, they are pervaded with a feeling of joy (Greek *chara*), which the Stoics called a "good passion" (Greek *eu-patheia*)—and which Paul has even turned into a major motif in his letter to the Philippians. In spite of all the afflictions one may experience in this world, Pauline Christ believers fundamentally *rejoice* in the consciousness that Christ (and all Christ believers who have received the pneuma) have *overcome* sin (i.e., the passions and the ensuing acts) and death (which, as Paul saw it, is the wages of sin). His claim in Galatians 5:24 (see in **T2.3**) that "those who belong to Christ Jesus have crucified the flesh with its passions and desires" is precisely matched by his reference two verses earlier (Gal 5:22) to joy as the second item on his list of pneumatic attitudes—just after love.

ACTUALIZATION

Until now, we have focused in chapters 1–2 on Paul's own ideas. But what should we ourselves make of all this? There is much in Paul that we cannot make our own, not least the whole cosmological picture that was Paul's: of the resurrection, the reception of a material pneuma, its effects, and much more. This in fact holds of the cosmological picture both in its specifically theological dimension (what God has done and will do) and in its specifically ethical dimension (concerning the effect of the pneuma on the lives of human beings with one another). A few so-called fundamentalist Christians may adhere to these ideas as part of their own understanding of the world, but by far the majority of Christians do not. This whole dimension of Paul's understanding is one that we must set aside. But even if we restrict ourselves to Paul's picture of the cognitive side of the specifically ethical dimension of life here and now, we may get into difficulties. Are we, for instance, able to make the radical altruism of Paul's maxim our own—*always* and *only* think of the good of others, *never* of your own?

Here it is important to see that this idea must present itself to us as what we call an ideal. Paul himself understood it quite differently: it was wholly real here and now through Christ faith and the reception of the pneuma. Not only were believers *meant* to live like that: they actually did! Inspired by Paul (and others), various religious virtuosi of a later age have attempted to put into practice this part of his worldview as literally understood. The monks of antiquity and the Middle Ages are one example. Think, for instance, of Saint Francis of Assisi (1181–1226). Parts of this attempt (but certainly not everything in it) may well be good and fine. Nevertheless, as I see it, after more than two thousand years of experimentation with this kind of rejection of human bodiliness and desire, we must say stop. We can neither believe in nor accept this kind of denial of our bodies and of our individuality. There is simply too much in our understanding of the way human beings think and feel that points in the direction of seeing them (us!) as being fundamentally and irremovably focused on ourselves and our bodies. Moreover, this focus on ourselves is in no way just bad. *We* cannot think of any state of salvation here and now that is not based in ourselves and in our bodies.

Is Paul's whole conception, then, just wrong or at most a beautiful utopian idea that is in the end superfluous? Not at all. Precisely as an ideal that articulates a *direction* for human feeling and action, it has the highest importance. An ideal is by definition impossible to reach and fulfill. Nevertheless, by articulating a criterion for human feeling and action in the form of a standard to which human beings may strive as a goal, the ideal contains a truth about human beings that is just as real as the fact that they will never *reach* the goal. Thus understood, what the Pauline ideal means, if we translate it into a modern way of understanding, is that the state of an irremovable focus on ourselves that is based on ourselves and our bodies *but also has a direction toward a shared community* is the true good for us, which is also the place of happiness and salvation.

What we may take over from Paul is neither his understanding of the negative starting point (*against* the body and the self) nor his understanding of the positive end point (*for* a complete altruism in a community of love). Rather, it is the idea of a *direction* for human feeling and action, one that *incorporates* the starting point—but then also moves in the direction of an end point where the importance for the individual of the body and the self is *lessened* in favor of a community in which there is *corresponding* room for others. Perhaps one may even say that *this* form of the community of love is the most real one: the community where there is room for *all*, with all our *own* body-based individualities.

In this way, we may in fact both understand and see the modern value of the Pauline idea of community of love in freedom—or perhaps better, of freedom in a community of love. We live in an age in which modern individualism has assumed the seat of honor, which makes each individual sufficient to him- or herself: *I* want to have *more* for my own body. At the same time, it is obvious that the massive climate problems with which we are confronted cry out for a shared community. If we want to include the whole of humanity in our understanding, we need to let us inspire by Paul in his attack on the works of the flesh (which focus on our own individual consumption) in favor of the fruit of the pneuma (which finds joy and happiness in trying to live *more* in accordance with Paul's maxim). In this way, we will ourselves give up *something* in order to let others get just as much—and perhaps let humanity recover its balance with the earth.

This kind of life will not focus exclusively on the community to the loss of all individuality. Perhaps Paul himself did not think so either. When *everybody* thinks of the good of *others*, there will in fact be room for every single one. This is a fascinating idea, which we will consider more closely in the following chapters. It also implies, however, that people will be free of their own individual desires and passions, where these are understood as resulting from a compulsive fixation on themselves. Here we find a genuine community of individuals in freedom. If we understand this as an ideal and a direction for human feeling and action, it is an idea that combines what we call socialism (the community) with what we call liberalism (freedom). It seems obvious that understood in this way, the Pauline idea of a community of love in freedom is highly relevant to our present-day political concerns.

3

THE OPPOSITION

CHRIST BELIEVERS, JEWS, AND PAGANS

IN HIS LETTERS, Paul again and again attempted to handle different kinds of opposition he had encountered in the congregations to which he was writing. In this chapter, we will look at the conflict over the question of how Paul's non-Jewish Christ believers should relate to the law of Moses. Should they keep the law? Or should they be indifferent to it? Some people said one thing; others the other. Enters Paul into this field with an overall position that is much more differentiated and interesting than that of his opponents. It is this position that we must attempt to grasp.

There is a follow-up question. If Christ-believing Jews declared, as they did in Galatians, that Christ-believing non-Jews should become Jews (by following the law of Moses), there would be no problem with the identity of the latter. Their ethnic identity would be clear. They would be Jews. Conversely, if the Christ-believing non-Jews declared, as they did in Romans, that Christ-believing non-Jews should be indifferent to the law of Moses, there would be no problem with *their* identity. They, too, would have a clear ethnic identity. They would (continue to) be non-Jews. However, if Paul on his side rejected either position, which identity did he ascribe to Christ believers? This question is relevant to both Christ-believing non-Jews *and* Jews even though Paul in his letters only addresses non-Jews and also primarily speaks of them. In short, Paul's way of handling how his non-Jewish Christ-believing addressees should relate to the law of Moses raises a central question about the identity of all Christ believers. Who and what were they by Paul's lights?

A DOUBLE OPPOSITION

Before we begin, we will do well to remind ourselves of two texts in Galatians that show the direction in which Paul aims to go. There is first Galatians 3:28 (see in **T0.14**):

> (**T0.14**) [28]There is *no longer Jew or Greek*, there is *no longer slave or free*, there is *no longer male and female*; for *all of you are one in Christ Jesus*.

Next, there is Galatians 5:6 (**T2.1**):

> (**T2.1**) [6]For in Christ Jesus neither circumcision nor uncircumcision counts for anything; the only thing that counts is faith working through love.

If they are *all* sons of God and one in Christ Jesus but also either Jews or non-Jews, then the question of their identity must be more complicated than in the view of Paul's opponents on either side, who took it that they will straightforwardly either be Jews or (continue to be) non-Jews. But what does the more complicated position look like? If they are *all* "one in Christ Jesus," does it not matter at all to Paul whether they are (also) either Jews or non-Jews?

As already noted, the views that Paul encountered on the issue of the relationship of his non-Jewish Christ believers to the law of Moses were diametrically opposed to one another in spite of the fact that Paul was everywhere writing to non-Jews. In Galatians, he argues intensely for the position that once the non-Jewish Galatians had converted to the Christ faith, they should *not* submit to the law of Moses, including acquiring an ethnic identity as Jews by letting themselves be circumcised (for the men, that is). Here

Paul's opponents were to begin with some Jewish Christ-believing preachers who had turned up among the Christ-believing Galatians once Paul, their founder, had left them. The newly arrived preachers had argued that the Galatians ought to take the full step: having converted to the Christ faith, they ought to become Jews by letting themselves be circumcised; after all, the Christ faith itself was a Jewish matter. In the second round, Paul's opponents are those among the Galatians themselves who had apparently been impressed by the newly arrived preachers. Paul reacts with anger: Non-Jews who converted to the Christ faith should *not* become Jews! Their Christ faith was *sufficient*! We must ask, Why is that? If the Christ faith was itself a Jewish matter, then why should the Galatians not take the full step? And what would their identity be as Christ believers but not Jews?

In 1 Corinthians and Romans, the position that Paul attempts to handle is diametrically opposed. Here, too, the congregations are made up of non-Jews who have become Christ believing. But here there are some members of the congregation who wish to *separate* themselves from Judaism. They have their freedom (from the law of Moses) in Christ and hence need not follow the various requirements of the law—for instance, on what one must and must not eat. Here, too, Paul reacts negatively, not quite so angrily, but nevertheless intensely. When their own freedom to eat anything means that their Jewish co-congregationalists are shocked, the non-Jewish Christ believers must *yield—even though* they are in principle right. Once again, we must ask why. If the non-Jewish Christ believers are in principle right, then why should they yield to their Jewish brothers and avoid eating the contested food? Were they, after all, expected to have an identity that verged on the Jewish one?

To answer these two questions, we must look carefully first at Galatians and next at 1 Corinthians and Romans. Behind it all lies the question of which identity Paul ends up constructing for his Christ-believing non-Jewish addressees—and, by implication, also for Christ-believing Jews.

GALATIANS: ARGUMENTS AGAINST LETTING THE LAW OF MOSES APPLY TO NON-JEWS

The letter to the Galatians is—next to 2 Corinthians—Paul's most intense letter. Here he really fears that his Galatian congregations are slipping away from him. He normally begins his letters by thanking God for the conversion of the congregation he is addressing. Here, however, he expresses strong surprise at them and even hurls maledictions against them (Gal 1:6–9):

> **T3.1** [6]I am astonished that you are so quickly deserting the one who called you in the grace of Christ and are turning to a different gospel—
> [7]which does not exist, but there are some who are confusing you and want to pervert the gospel of Christ. [8]But even if we [Paul himself] or an angel from heaven should proclaim to you a gospel contrary to what we proclaimed to you, let that one be accursed! [9]As we have said before, so now I repeat, if anyone proclaims to you a gospel contrary to what you received, let that one be accursed!

A little later, he says this (3:1; 4:12–15, 19–20):

> **T3.2** [3:1]You foolish Galatians! Who has bewitched you? It was before your eyes that Jesus Christ was publicly exhibited [namely, in Paul himself] as crucified! . . . [4:12]Friends, I beg you, become as I am, for I also have become as you are. You have done me no wrong.
> [13]You know that it was because of a physical infirmity that I first announced the gospel to you; [14]though my condition put you to the test, you did not scorn or despise me, but welcomed me as an angel of God, as Christ Jesus. [15]What has become of the goodwill you felt? For I testify that, had it been possible, you would have torn out your eyes and given them to me. . . . [19]My little children, for whom I am again in the pain of childbirth until Christ is formed in you, [20]I wish

> I were present with you now and could change my tone, for I am perplexed about you.

Why does Paul appeal so strongly to the Galatians' original conversion and enthusiasm for him? We already know the answer: the Christ faith was meant to be *sufficient* for them. That is precisely his conclusion in Galatians 5:6 (**T2.1**) once he has argued that the Christ-believing non-Jewish Galatians are free of the law of Moses (5:1, see in **T2.11**). But we also remember from Galatians 5:13–25 (**T2.2** and **T2.3**) the further point that having acquired Christ faith, the non-Jewish Galatians will receive the pneuma and, through that means, also those attitudes that make them always act in *accordance* with the law of Moses (without having *submitted* to it, that is). They actually *fulfill* it. In this almost paradoxical manner, the law of Moses has *itself* become superfluous for them. What they must hold on to is *only* their Christ faith. That is fully sufficient.

Still, why is it that they should not also take the full step and become Jews (by being circumcised) so that they might also come to live *directly* under the law? That, it seems, would remove the anomaly of their not *submitting* to the law *but* fulfilling it. Paul's answer as given in **T2.1** is that whether one lives under the law of Moses (by being circumcised) or not (by being uncircumcised) *does not matter*. Even more, it *must* not matter. For if it does matter—that is, if human beings themselves *allow* it to matter—then they will thereby remove some of the weight from the *only* thing that matters for justice and salvation: Christ faith. By submitting to the law, the non-Jewish Christ believers will necessarily give *some* importance for justice and salvation to the law. But as Paul has intensely argued, it has none! Only one thing does: the Christ faith, which is both a necessary and sufficient condition for justice and salvation. There is here a single thing that is itself *common* to Jews and non-Jews. Nothing else must have any independent significance.

Please, do not forget that Paul was a faith fanatic. What we meet here is his crucial claim. Only one thing brings justice and salvation: Christ faith. Other things (e.g., whether one is ethnically a Jew or a non-Jew) may well play a role for one's self-understanding (we will come back to that), but they have no real significance for what the whole thing is all about: justice and salvation. They are (as we may say) *indifferent* for salvation. Paul here makes use of a way of thinking that is also found in Greco-Roman philosophy—in particular, Stoicism. Only one thing is necessary for salvation (or in Stoicism, only one thing is genuinely good); all other things are "indifferent" (Greek *adiaphora*) for salvation (or in Stoicism, for happiness). We will meet this way of thinking again and again. I call it Paul's "double model." What it means is that the indifferent things are on the one hand literally wholly indifferent in relation to salvation and happiness but on the other hand also not *completely* indifferent. In Stoicism, only one thing (namely, moral virtue) is genuinely good and leads to happiness, but other things—like health, wealth, and material goods—though indifferent for happiness may well be "preferable": "to be taken" (as they said) *if* that is allowed for by the only thing that genuinely matters. Similarly, for Christ-believing Jews in antiquity, it might well have a certain significance for their self-understanding that they were ethnically Jews. The same would hold for the ethnic self-understanding of Christ-believing non-Jews. That would then be all right. Only, for Paul, it was not this that mattered *at all* in relation to justice and salvation. In that relation, one's ethnic status was wholly indifferent. Similarly, for the Stoics, it was not the ordinary "goods" that mattered at all in relation to happiness. In that relation, *they* were wholly indifferent.

We already know that Paul developed a genuine argument (in Gal 5:6 and 5:13–25, **T2.1–3**) for this claim with regard to the ethical side of the matter. Christ faith, which one might have independently of whether one was a Jew or a non-Jew and which led to reception of the pneuma, was in itself *sufficient* to make believers live in relation to one another in the way they should. For this, nothing else was in fact necessary. Hence one should not require anything else in addition.

That argument pertains to the ethical side of the matter. Earlier in Galatians, Paul has also developed an argument with the same conclusion with regard to the theological side—that is, concerning the relationship with Christ and God. Here, too, Christ faith is both necessary and sufficient. The text (Gal 2:14–21), which is both compact and striking, is one more example of Paul's linguistic genius. In what immediately precedes it (from Gal 2:11), he has described how on a special occasion in the Syrian city of Antioch, his apostolic colleague Peter avoided—as a Jew—eating together with the non-Jewish Christ believers present, apparently out of concern for some other Jews who were also present. Paul had criticized Peter for this at the time (2:15–16), and he now (2:17–21) develops his position into something that is directly relevant to his Galatian addressees. Here is the whole text:

> **T3.3** [14]If you [Peter], though a Jew, live like a Gentile and not like a Jew, how can you compel the Gentiles to live like Jews? [15]We ourselves [both you and I] are Jews by birth and not Gentile sinners; [16]yet knowing that a person is justified not by the works of the law but through faith in Jesus Christ, we have come to believe in Christ Jesus, so that we might be justified by faith in Christ, and not by doing the works of the law, because no one will be justified by the works of the law. [17]But if, in our effort to be justified in Christ, we ourselves have been found [by other Jews] to be sinners, is Christ then a servant of sin? Certainly not! [18]But if I [i.e., you, Peter!] build up again the very things that I [i.e., you] once tore down [namely, the law], then I [i.e., you] demonstrate that I [you] am a transgressor [namely, of the law]. [19]I, by contrast [i.e., Paul himself]

> have died to the law through the law, so that I might live to God. I have been crucified with Christ; [20]and it is no longer I who live, but it is Christ who lives in me. And to the extent that I now live in the flesh, I live in faith, faith in the Son of God, who loved me and gave himself for me. [21]I do not nullify the grace of God; for if justification came through the law, then Christ died for nothing.

There are two main points in this. First (2:15–16), Peter and Paul had together realized that nobody is made just by works of the law—that is, by (trying to) live in accordance with the law alone. Something else was necessary: Christ faith. Second (2:19–21), Paul describes what this realization had meant in his own case: that he (though a Jew) had died to the law of Moses by, as it were, being crucified together with Christ in such a way that to the extent that he is still physically alive, he lives in Christ faith alone. It is *Christ* and Christ *alone* who lives in Paul.

What Paul is describing here is a complete takeover of himself by Christ. We already know from chapter 1 how this should be understood in concrete terms. On the one hand, Paul came to have faith in Jesus Christ; on the other hand, he also received in his own body Christ's pneuma, which is also Christ himself. Seen in that light, one can immediately understand why nothing else mattered to him in relation to justice and salvation. Paul *himself* (the "sarkic" Paul) was no longer there. If one considers the matter in relation to the question of identity, the result is the same: *Paul* was no longer present. *In* "him," there was only Christ. Or the other way round, *he* was to be found only *in* Christ (compare Gal 3:26–28, **T0.14**). For Paul and the other Christ believers, then, one must primarily speak of a "Christ identity."

Thus both ethically and theologically, Paul understood the significance for Christ believers of Jesus Christ in such a way that nothing else would matter for justice and salvation. And hence, it *must* not matter either. Were that to happen, the significance of Jesus

Christ's death and resurrection would be diminished and dislocated. Then "Christ would have died for nothing" (Gal 2:21, see in **T3.3**).

Against the opponents among the Galatians (and those behind them) who thought that the Galatians should take the full step and submit to the law of Moses, thereby becoming Jews, Paul therefore argued with great intensity that the law of Moses was superfluous for non-Jews. Christ faith was itself sufficient for justice and salvation. In addition, the law of Moses was *already* fulfilled by Christ believers who had received the pneuma. Thus Jews and non-Jews were on an equal footing in relation to salvation. The question of their ethnic identity was without any significance at all and wholly indifferent in that respect.

It accords well with this position that Paul does not conversely argue that Christ believers who are ethnically Jews should *give up* being Jews. They might well continue to live in accordance with the law of Moses. Only, they must not either attach any real significance to their ethnic identity in relation to what alone mattered for justice and salvation: Christ faith. "For in Christ Jesus, neither circumcision nor uncircumcision counts for anything; the only thing that counts is faith working through love" (Gal 5:6, **T2.1**).

The result of this argument is that we must primarily speak of a Christ identity for believers, both Jews and non-Jews. But what, then, does "primarily" mean here? Exactly how are the two types of identity—Christ and ethnic—related to one another? We will come back to this.

FIRST CORINTHIANS AND ROMANS: ARGUMENTS ON WHY THE LAW OF MOSES MAY CONTINUE TO REMAIN IN FORCE FOR JEWS

Both 1 Corinthians and Romans are addressed to Christ believers who were not Jews. Here, however, the problem is not that these people wanted to become Jews. On the contrary, they wanted to turn their back on Judaism. That will not do either, says Paul. Well, didn't he just say that . . . ?

First Corinthians is a richly faceted letter. In three chapters (1 Cor 8–10), Paul discusses a question with which the Corinthian believers have apparently been much concerned. If they were invited to dinner by their non-Christ-believing and non-Jewish friends, were they allowed to eat whatever meat was served, since this might well be "sacrificial meat" coming from animals that had been sacrificed to heathen gods in a temple? As so often, Paul's answer is twofold. On the one hand, Yes, the Corinthians might well eat that kind of meat. His argument is striking (1 Cor 8:4–6):

> **T3.4** [4]As to the eating of food offered to idols, we know that "no idol in the world really exists," and that "there is no God but one." [5]Indeed, even though there may be so-called gods in heaven or on earth—as in fact there are many gods and many lords—[6]yet for us there is one God, the Father, from whom are all things and for whom we exist, and one Lord, Jesus Christ, through whom are all things and through whom we exist.

The conclusion must be that one may very well eat sacrificial meat—since "for us" idols do not at all exist!

However, things are not quite so easy. Some members of the congregation have not (yet) been able to free themselves of the sense that idols do exist. Their conscience, says Paul, is "weak" (8:7), and it will be "defiled" (the opposite of having a good conscience) if either they themselves or other members of the congregation eat the contested meat. What to do about that?

In its essence, Paul's answer is as follows. The strong Christ believers with a good conscience are in principle right. Nevertheless, they must take care not to become a stumbling block (8:9) to the weak because of their own right to eat meat that is (at least, potentially) sacrificial meat. They must therefore *renounce* employing the right that they do have—out of consideration for the weak. As Paul says a little later in the same connection (10:23)—and we know it already (**T2.14**)—"'All things are permitted,' but not all things are beneficial. 'All things are permitted,' but not all things *build up*."

Note also that he makes an important addition (10:24), which actually repeats his maxim from Philippians 2:4 (see in **T2.5**):

> **T3.5** [24]Do not seek your own advantage, *but* that of the other.

In the case at hand, those who take offense when Christ believers eat sacrificial meat risk becoming non-believers. So much the more must the strong Christ believers show consideration for them—for their sake but not for their own. For as Paul adds concerning the strong (10:29–30),

> **T3.6** [29]Why should my liberty be subject to the judgment of someone else's conscience? [30]If I partake with thankfulness, why should I be denounced because of that for which I give thanks?

The argument may appear contrived. Is one's own conscience, to be understood as one's relationship with God when one eats the contested meat, in fact sufficient to justify and allow one to eat it? The answer is a resounding yes! That is precisely what is at stake. It all depends on the inner attitude. *Nevertheless*, the strong Christ believers must renounce employing the right that is actually theirs. For here there is an even stronger principle that applies: Paul's maxim (see in **T2.5**).

Paul may therefore conclude more generally as follows, once more repeating his maxim (10:31–11:1):

> **T3.7** [10:31]So, whether you eat or drink, or whatever you do, do everything for the glory of God. [32]Give no offense to Jews or to Greeks or to the church of God, [33]just as I try to please everyone in

> everything I do, *not seeking my own advantage, but that of the many*, so that they may be saved. [11:1]Be imitators of me, as I am of Christ.

Christ is the great model by whose example Paul himself lives (see 9:19–23, **T2.13**). When there is some particular issue that needs to be taken into consideration—be it in relation to Jews or Greeks or within the congregation—Christ believers must follow the same example. In the present case, they must *give up* their freedom and the right that is in principle theirs of eating anything they wish.

In Romans 14–15 (14:1–15:6), it becomes even clearer that this attitude must be adopted—specifically in relation to *Jewish* Christ-believing members of the congregation who, in view of the requirements of the Mosaic law, are concerned when their non-Jewish co-congregationalists are prepared to eat anything whatsoever. At first, Paul insists (as in 1 Cor) that all people are allowed to eat or not to eat whatever they wish as long as they do so "for the Lord" (Rom 14:6):

> **T3.8** [6]Those who eat, eat in honor of the Lord, since they give thanks to God; while those who abstain, abstain in honor of the Lord and give thanks to God.

Paul immediately justifies this principle (14:7–9):

> **T3.9** [7]We do not live to ourselves, and we do not die to ourselves. [8]If we live, we live to the Lord, and if we die, we die to the Lord; so then, whether we live or whether we die, we are the Lord's. [9]For to this end Christ died and lived again, so that he might be Lord of both the dead and the living.

In short, it is all about one's relationship with Christ and God. Seen in that context, it is completely indifferent whether one eats this or that.

Nevertheless, Paul goes on to take half of this back again by using a characteristic wordplay on "judging" (14:13–15):

> **T3.10** [13]Let us therefore no longer pass judgment on one another, but judge this instead: never to put a stumbling block or hindrance in the way of another. [14]I [myself] know and am persuaded in the Lord Jesus that nothing is unclean in itself; but it is unclean for anyone who thinks it unclean. [15]Therefore, if your brother is being injured by what you eat, you are no longer walking in love. Do not let what you eat cause the ruin of one for whom Christ died.

The idea is that if the weak members of the congregation are concerned about what their stronger brothers eat, then the weak ones risk losing their unique and direct focus on Christ. Will they then at all get a share in the resurrection for which Christ stands? Will it all not end in their ruin (namely, eternal death)? Thus if the strong insist on their right, they will no longer let themselves be led by *agapê* (love), which, according to Paul's maxim, should govern all their acts. Even though a Jewish member of the congregation may not have left the requirements of the law behind, his non-Jewish brother must give up on his own right. Paul therefore concludes his whole discussion by once more introducing his maxim of never thinking of oneself. And as he does at the end of **T3.10**, he even brings in his strongest card, Christ's own death and resurrection (15:1–3):

> **T3.11** [1]We who are strong ought to put up with the failings of the weak, and not to please ourselves. [2]Each of us must please our neighbor for the good purpose of building up the neighbor. [3]For Christ did not please himself.

It is clear that in both 1 Corinthians and Romans, Paul is discussing the same issue of eating meat that is potentially sacrificial meat. All the more noteworthy is the fact that it is not altogether clear in the two letters exactly who the weak people are who are concerned about the issue. In 1 Corinthians, the weak are not necessarily Jewish Christ believers. They might also be non-Jewish Christ believers who had not yet given up completely their belief that what Paul calls idols (their own previous gods) do exist (compare **T3.4**), which would then have consequences for the meat that might have been sacrificed to those idols. In Romans, it is clearer that Paul's target is Jewish Christ believers in particular. For Jews, the pagan gods were idols, *lesser* gods than the Jewish God but still gods. Could one then eat meat that had potentially been sacrificed to them? What is noteworthy about this lack of clarity with regard to Paul's target is the fact that he might make use of the same argument in either case. On the one hand, whether or not idols exist, "for us" only God and Christ do exist. No matter what one therefore eats, it will be wholly unproblematic to do so as long as one eats in honor of God. This is Paul's theological claim. It holds for both Jewish and non-Jewish Christ believers. On the other hand, it is also the case that *if* there are members in the congregation who are concerned over this issue, then it is Paul's maxim that holds. This rule, too, he has developed from his theological claim about the purpose of Christ's coming, and it stands *above* the other one. Paul manages to articulate this point with gusto in both letters—in 1 Corinthians 10:31–11:1 (**T3.7**) and in Romans 14:17:

> **T3.12** 17For the kingdom of God is not food and drink but righteousness and peace and joy in holy pneuma!

What matters is not what one does but the attitude behind it—and here in particular this attitude as it comes to expression in one's relationship with others as governed by Paul's maxim.

When we turn to the question of what kind of identity Paul is constructing for his addressees, we will see the central importance of the fact that his argument over eating the contested meat has two dimensions to it. In the first place, it holds for both Jewish and non-Jewish Christ believers. In both cases, the strong in the congregation must renounce their right and yield to perceptions among the weak that reflect their identities before they became Christ believers. In the second place, Paul's argument shows the central importance of the attitude behind what one does (namely, whether one eats), not just in relation to the act itself, but also in relation to other Christ believers who are involved in the matter. When I began to read Paul, I was surprised to see that he spends so much time and energy on the very specific question of whether one might eat meat that is potentially sacrificial meat. That surprise was misplaced. For the question not only concerns the practical issue of the relationship of Christ believers to the immediately surrounding world when they have been invited to dinner. It also concerns much more broadly the two religious traditions—the Jewish and the non-Jewish one—that in different ways run together in Paul's understanding of Christ faith. Also, the question shows the central importance of the inner attitude with regard to external acts. Paul manages to articulate this idea with considerable force in his argument. It is in this idea that we will find his understanding of Christ identity.

THE NARROW PATH OF TRUTH

We have seen how in Galatians and 1 Corinthians and Romans, Paul handled some opponents in the congregations who were moving in two diametrically opposed directions. In Galatians, they wanted to submit directly to the law of Moses. In 1 Corinthians and (at least) in Romans, they wanted to leave the law completely behind. Both were wrong as Paul saw it. As non-Jews (the Galatians), they were entirely free of the law of Moses and must not submit directly to it. But as non-Jews (the Corinthians and Romans), they were nevertheless not allowed to employ their freedom in such a way that it might lead their (possibly)

Jewish co-congregationalists to their downfall. What holds these two positions together is the idea that the *only* thing that matters is Christ faith working through love (Gal 5:6, **T2.1**)—*in combination with* Paul's maxim of always thinking of the good of others (Phil 2:4, see in **T2.5**), which is precisely what Pauline love consists in. Whether one is a Jew (circumcised) or a non-Jew (uncircumcised) is indifferent. Whether one eats one thing or the other is indifferent. The only things that have any significance are Jesus Christ and Christ faith (theology)—*and* the ethics that springs from that: working through love. This ethics, of which Christ's death on the cross was itself the most striking example, urges Christ believers to yield to all others who cannot themselves understand it in its full, radical form. *Above* all individual identity markers, which create boundaries between human beings, there is a single identity-creating value that finds expression in a disregard for *one's own* individual identity markers (including ethnic ones), where this is required by the consideration for the others. This is the full form of Paul's use of his double model.

What, then, is the actual role—if any—of the individual identity markers in this picture? They may well be indifferent in relation to justice and salvation. But are they also wholly indifferent in relation to people's sense of their own identities? As promised, we will come back to this question.

PAUL AND JUDAISM

We have seen that Paul, on the one hand, was intensely against the idea that his non-Jewish Christ believers should become Jews and, on the other hand, also demanded that the same Christ believers must show consideration for their Jewish co-congregationalists. What, then, is the relationship between Christ faith and Judaism in all this? Did Christ faith differ from Judaism in Paul's mind so that we here have an altogether new "religion," what we might call "Christianity"? Or was Christ faith, rather, a new form *of* Judaism in such a way that there is absolutely no new religion here?

The answer is, I believe, simple even though it has created huge problems both to understand and accept it. There are two points. First, the Pauline Christ faith *is* Jewish—even more, in Paul's mind, it was, by now, the only true form of Judaism. With the arrival of the Messiah in the figure of Jesus Christ, Judaism had—in the mind of Paul, the apocalypticist—reached its end point. The Jews lived no longer in the era of the law of Moses but in that of Christ—when the law of Moses would at long last be *fulfilled*. What was to follow (and very soon!) was a resurrection to life in heaven that was also prefigured in other versions of Jewish apocalyptic thinking. That is the first point. The second is that understood in this way, Judaism became accessible on an equal footing to all, irrespective of their traditional ethnicity. The non-Jews were not meant to become Jews by conforming to all the *traditional* ethnic markers that made a Jew a Jew. If they did, that move would dislocate the focus from the only thing that would bring justice and salvation: Christ. In spite of that, through their Christ faith, they were parts—together with the Jewish Christ believers—in a single shared entity: true Judaism (the first point), but now consisting of both Jewish and non-Jewish Christ believers (the second point). In relation to this entity, the traditional ethnic markers (e.g., being circumcised or not) were indifferent. They might well continue to be there, but they did not matter. For true Judaism was defined by one thing alone: Christ faith. Paul shows in two places in Romans (2 and 11) exactly how non-Jewish and Jewish Christ believers, respectively, will be part of true Judaism. Since the notion of true Judaism is strongly contested among contemporary readers of Paul, we will look a bit more closely at these passages.

In Romans 1–3 (1:18–3:20), Paul aims to show that "all, both Jews and Greeks [namely, before or outside Christ faith] are under sin" (3:9). In chapter 1, this is shown to hold of non-Jews; in chapter 2, it gradually comes to hold also of Jews. Paul summarizes the result of this in a striking text (Rom 2:25–29), which is one more example of his linguistic genius (and daring!):

> **T3.13** [25]Circumcision indeed is of value if you practice the law; but if you break the law, your circumcision has become uncircumcision. [26]So, if those who are uncircumcised keep the requirements of the law, will not their uncircumcision be reckoned as circumcision? [27]Then those who are physically uncircumcised but keep the law will condemn you [Jews] who have the written code and circumcision but also break the law. [28]For a Jew is not the one who is so outwardly, nor is circumcision the one that is so outwardly in the flesh. [29]Rather, *a Jew is the one who is so inwardly*, and *circumcision is a matter of the heart*, in the pneuma and not literal. Such a person receives praise not from others but from God.

In this text, Paul claims two things. First, circumcision—and hence Judaism—is a matter of whether one *acts* in accordance with the law of Moses. We already know the underlying idea from Galatians 5:13–25 (**T2.2–3**): reception of the pneuma makes a person fulfill the law of Moses by issuing in a set of other-regarding attitudes that will in fact make the person act in accordance with the requirements of the law. In the Galatians text, Paul was speaking of non-Jews, who were not under the law. In the present text, he is speaking of Jews and claiming—with the logic of his argument—that they only *are* Jews if they actually *practice* the law. In this way, Paul is unmistakably beginning to reinterpret what constitutes Judaism. Only those Jews who *practice* the law are real or true Jews—as it were, *the* Jews.

Second, the type of attitude that issues in the proper acts may also be found in people who have not been physically circumcised—that is, in (traditional) non-Jews. In that case, their uncircumcision should be *reckoned as* circumcision. If we take the latter claim seriously, what it means is that they, the physically uncircumcised non-Jews, now *are* Jews. They are not just *like* the (real) Jews: they *are* Jews, as these are now to be understood. In these two ways, Paul produces a thorough reinterpretation of what constitutes Judaism. It is all a matter of *practicing* the law no matter whether one is under it or not.

The conclusion to Paul's argument comes in 2:28–29 in the form of a startling claim: being a Jew and being circumcised is in fact now a matter of something interior in the heart, not of something exterior; it is a matter of pneuma, not of flesh (sarx). By this last claim, Paul shows that in the argument of 2:25–29, he is in fact talking of Christ faith and Christ believers. He has begun (chapter 1) talking of non-Jews outside Christ and continued (eventually, in chapter 2) talking of Jews outside Christ. When he intends to summarize in the present text what he is *positively* after—namely, the attitude that means that the law of Moses is *done*—he in fact speaks of Christ believers. They alone have the pneuma. And they alone are now Jews.

In our context, the point is that **T3.13** clearly shows that through Christ faith and reception of the pneuma, non-Jews *become Jews where it really matters*: inwardly, with a circumcision of the heart. One might say that they are "honorary" Jews. In terms of the traditional criteria for being a Jew, they are not Jews, but in terms of what has turned out to be *the single true criterion of Judaism*, they are. I repeat, by the new light of what makes a person a Jew, the non-Jewish Christ believers now *are* Jews. Paul has here constructed a different and true form of Judaism, one that consists of *all* (and only) those who—through Christ faith—*fulfill* the law of Moses.

But he also does something more. By describing both Jewish and non-Jewish Christ believers as the real Jews, he shows himself to be operating with two levels of understanding that directly reflect his double model as we already know it. By now, the traditional ethnic differences between Jews and non-Jews, which continue to be there, have been demoted to a lower level of identity markers that no longer genuinely matter for being a Jew. By contrast, there is an upper level of being a real Jew, to which both (traditional) Jews *and* (traditional) non-Jews belong when they have acquired Christ faith. This level gives them all *the same* identity: Jewish Christ identity. At the lower level, the traditional differences of identity between Jews and non-Jews *remain* in place. *Only* (and this is the point of the double model with its two levels), the traditional differences do not *matter* for the identity that they all share: Jewish Christ identity.

Exactly how should we understand Paul's traditionally Jewish Christ believers (including himself!) in relation to this notion of true Judaism? The answer is already implicit in the text just quoted (**T3.13**). They must be *like* the (non-Jewish) honorary Jews by having what makes *them* honorary Jews: Christ faith and pneuma so that they will in fact fulfill the Mosaic law. In their case, too, that is the only thing that genuinely matters for their identity. By contrast, their traditional identity as Jews (however important it may seem to them and although it remains in place) has by now been demoted to the lower level.

The resulting overall picture is one that Paul sets forth most explicitly in Romans chapters 9–11, where chapter 11 is especially revealing. The question he aims to answer in these chapters is why his Jewish compatriots have not joined the Christ faith. Answer: the non-Jews (namely, the Christ believers among them) were meant to come in first, but the Jews will soon follow even though they do not yet believe in Christ. What will the result of all this then look like? Paul invents an image in order to visualize the answer (11:16–24). He speaks of an olive tree that has a fat root—and of branches that are broken off and others that are grafted in. The central point is that the olive tree into which they will *all* (traditional Jews as well as traditional non-Jews) be grafted as its branches (instead of those that have been broken off) has a fat root that is capable of carrying the whole tree. That root stands for Judaism in the form in which

Paul has described it in 9:4–5: those to whom belong "the adoption, the glory, the covenants, the giving of the law, the worship, and the promises" and also "the patriarchs and . . . the Messiah." Christ-believing non-Jews, who have originally come from a wild olive tree, have already been grafted into the natural tree. By contrast, non-Christ-believing Jews have been broken off from the same tree. But God will once again graft them in. The result will be the Jewish, natural olive tree with two sets of branches: some (originally non-Jewish) branches that have been grafted into it for the first time, thereby becoming parts of the Jewish tree, and some old (and originally Jewish) branches that originally belonged to it *but have been grafted into it once more.*

Here, too, we see how Paul attempts to follow the narrow path of truth between various types of one-sidedness on either side of the path: not the non-Jews as they *were*—but neither the Jews as *they* were. In the middle, between these two parties, the new olive tree towers in the shape of Christ-believing Judaism, a tree that on the one hand is old (namely, Jewish) and on the other hand has branches that are *all new*: non-Jewish branches that have been grafted in for the first time and Jewish branches that have been grafted in once more. This tree constitutes what is *now* the true Judaism. And of course it has a gardener who is in charge of breaking off old branches, grafting in new ones, and so on. That gardener is the Jewish God.

Paul has spoken metaphorically. How should we understand his image more specifically with regard to the question of identity? The tree itself, as we noted, stands for Judaism, but now as identified by Christ faith, which Paul had *also* included in his account of Judaism in 9:4–5. The people who have been grafted in but were originally non-Jews are now also (real) Jews—although honorary Jews, since they have not been there all the time. Still, the fact that they are now Christ-believing Jews is the central thing about their identity. It belongs to the upper level. Do they also continue to be non-Jews in ethnic terms at the lower level? Yes, since they must not let themselves be circumcised, they continue to be non-Jews by traditional ethnic standards. However, this status is (as we know) *indifferent* in relation to their justice and salvation and hence also to their real identity. They now *are* what in Paul's metaphor are the (*originally* wild) branches that have been grafted into the natural tree of Judaism. Though only honorary Jews in terms of the traditional ethnic standards, in Paul's view, they now are *true* Jews, Christ-believing Jews.

How, then, about those represented in the metaphor by the original branches, both those who by having Christ faith continue to belong to the tree of Judaism (like Paul himself) and those who were momentarily broken off, since they had not (yet) acquired Christ faith, but would then be grafted in once more (as Paul foresees)? These people continue to be Jews by traditional standards. But in their case, too, their traditional status is *indifferent* to justice and salvation and also to their real identity. What gives them this identity is the fact that they are Christ-believing (Jews). In this way, too, they are evidently Jews. For Christ faith is Judaism. But it now also holds that due to their Christ faith, they *share* their identity (namely, the *truly* Jewish one) with the originally non-Jewish believers. They, too, are now *true* Jews, Christ-believing Jews.

Christ-believing Jews—that is what both the originally non-Jewish and the originally Jewish Christ believers now are at the upper level. But a question remains, to which we have repeatedly referred.

THE IDENTITY OF CHRIST BELIEVERS

The question is this: What role (if any) does their *original* (but now lower-level) status as non-Jews or Jews, respectively, play for their identity? This question is central for the whole agenda of this book: to show that Paul's understanding of the relationship between ethnicity and identity is directly relevant to our own modern reflection on identity politics. (However, the contemporary side of this issue will only be addressed directly in the conclusion.)

Consider first the originally Jewish Christ believers. They may continue to be Jewish in a traditional, ethnic sense. They may follow the law of Moses, let themselves be circumcised, worship God in the temple in Jerusalem, and so on. But we saw that they must also recognize and constantly remind themselves that the *only* thing that matters for their salvation *and* identity as Jews is the Christ faith (itself a Jewish matter), which they completely share with their non-Jewish brothers. In other words, when one asks about their identity in relation to their non-Jewish brothers in Christ, their special, traditional, ethnic identity markers become completely irrelevant. *In spite of that*, however, if they are unable to leave completely behind their previous sense that their traditional practices (e.g., eating practices) matter, then their non-Jewish brothers must not *insist* that they should stop practicing them. Instead, *by* the Christ faith itself and the principle of love that is articulated in Paul's maxim, the non-Jews must let their Jewish brothers continue to behave the way they feel. Only, as Paul keeps insisting, those practices no longer genuinely matter. That is what he so carefully explains in Romans 14–15.

This will hold of the Jewish Christ believers who after having been broken off will eventually be grafted into the olive true once more. But it will also hold of those Jews (like Paul himself) who in the present constitute a "remnant" among the Jews: those who have *already* accepted the Christ faith (Rom 11:1–6). They have been Jews from the beginning and continue to be so without a break. But because of the change in Judaism caused by the coming of Christ, their Jewish identity will lie exclusively in their (Jewish) Christ faith and hence in what they share with their non-Jewish brothers in Christ. In their case, too, the traditional, ethnic identity markers that they may continue to exhibit have become completely irrelevant to the identity that matters. That is what Paul so strikingly claims in 1 Corinthians

(9:19–23, **T2.13**) to have shown in his own practice toward non-Jews and Jews, respectively. Here, too, however, we should say that were such Jews to feel in some way bound by their earlier practices (which, by **T2.13**, is unlikely in Paul's own case), then they would be free to do so as long as they did not take them to genuinely matter.

Consider then the originally non-Jewish Christ believers. They may in principle continue to live as non-Jews, and they *must* do so in relation to the law of Moses, to which they must not submit. However, being honorary Jews, there is one point where they have definitively left behind their earlier status as non-Jews. They have, as Paul already said in 1 Thessalonians (1:9–10, see in **T0.3**), "turned to [the Jewish] God *from idols*, to serve a living and true God, and to wait for his Son from heaven, whom he raised from the dead—Jesus, who rescues us from the wrath that is coming." As far as the worship of God goes, there is no road back for the non-Jewish Christ believers. That is what makes them honorary *Jews*. *Below* that level, however, they may well continue to live in their traditional ways—for example, by eating meat that may be "sacrificial"—as long as they do not attach any importance to them.

The result is complicated if one considers the traditional ethnic identity markers. The Jewish Christ believers may continue to live the way they have always done, *but* they must not ascribe any significance whatsoever to their traditional ethnicity. The non-Jewish Christ believers similarly can (and with regard to the law of Moses must) continue to live the way they have always done, *but* on a single point (regarding their worship of God), they must *not* continue as before. However, if one considers the two groups from above, everything falls into place. They *share* the Christ faith, and it is precisely because of their Christ faith that they must relate to their original ethnic identity markers in two different ways. The Jewish Christ believers must not—as we may say—attach any *religious* (i.e., god-regarding) significance to the law of Moses, for their own God has generated something *other* (namely, Christ) that is all-important. From now on, *that* is what gives them their identity. Similarly, the non-Jewish Christ believers must revise completely their *religious* (i.e., god-regarding) bonds—and for the same reason. And that is what from now on gives them their identity. The single all-important thing that both groups completely share is the Christ faith.

This way of understanding Paul places him right in the middle of two extremes on either side. On the one hand, there is a traditional, Christian interpretation, according to which Paul's idea of Christ faith was no longer a part of Judaism but stood for something entirely new: Christianity. Here the pendulum moved Paul entirely away from Judaism, and any Christ-believing Jews were no longer to be considered Jews. (They had "converted.") On the other hand, there is a modern, Jewish interpretation, according to which Paul's idea of Christ faith was very much a part of Judaism—only since Judaism was and remained ethnically defined by the law of Moses, the non-Jewish Christ believers remained somewhat anomalous: Christ believers *but* in fact outside of Judaism. Here the pendulum has moved Paul to the other extreme of favoring Jewish Christ believers over non-Jewish ones, since only the former have an identity that is entirely clear.

In the middle lies the Pauline position. It definitely sees Christ faith as Judaism—indeed, the true form of Judaism. And so Paul belongs squarely *within* Judaism. But it also places (traditional) Jews and non-Jews on an entirely equal footing with regard to justice, salvation, and their ultimate identity as Christ-believing Jews at the upper level. At the same time, it also requires *some* adjustment on both sides when it demotes the (religious) significance of non-Jewish gods (for traditional non-Jews) *and* the law of Moses (for traditional Jews) to the lower level of things that do not ultimately matter but where there is a certain degree of laissez-faire. Indeed, such laissez-faire is even required by the Christ faith itself as Paul interprets it in his maxim.

This Pauline position is a daring one, since it relies crucially on the idea of a reinterpretation of Judaism. We may well ask, Can one in this way just "reinterpret" what it is to be a Jew? One can therefore easily understand why the Pauline position was later interpreted by Christians in a Christian direction that left the Jewish dimension behind—and why it was similarly rejected by Jews, for whom the law of Moses was and remained the crucial identity marker for being a Jew.

However, it is crucial to see that this only happened *after* Paul when the ways between "Christianity" and "Judaism" had parted. In themselves, the two opposed positions are in fact already represented in the Pauline letters but as positions Paul rejects. The "Christian" one consists of those non-Jewish Christ believers in Romans who did not care for their Jewish brothers (Rom 11:18–24; 14:1–15:6). The "Jewish" position consists of the Jewish Christ believers in Galatia who sought to persuade the non-Jewish but already Christ-believing Galatians to let themselves be circumcised. Paul himself accepted neither position. He walked on the narrow path of truth, which is *a very thin line* right in the middle: fully Jewish and within Judaism to the one (Jewish) side but also such that Paul might eventually, against all his inmost wishes, be torn over to the other side by (non-Jewish) *Christians once* the connection with Judaism had been severed that Paul took for granted and for which he fought so intensely. In between these two positions, there *is* a line: that of Jewish Christ faith exemplified by Paul's metaphor of the olive tree of Judaism with a towering Christ at the top.

But the question remains: How can one in Paul's way just "reinterpret" what it is to be a Jew? Here, however, we should remember that Paul was a faith fanatic—moreover, one who expected Christ to return any moment. Paul had come to see Judaism itself differently and the whole global situation much more urgently. For him, the crucial identity marker was (the Jewish) Christ faith that would bring salvation in a moment. And he clearly saw the implications of this for (traditional) non-Jews too: they, too, might now become real Jews and reap the benefits of this wholly new situation. That was what turned this Jewish apostle for Christ into an apostle to non-Jews.

* * *

Is what we find in Paul, then, a universalism that transcends ethnic boundaries? That has been the traditional view, and as we noted in the introduction, it is an idea that the French philosopher Alain Badiou has turned into the core of his reading of Paul. The answer is both yes and no. Yes, ethnic boundaries were in fact transcended when both Jews and non-Jews were able to be one in Christ in exactly the same way, which meant that the traditional ethnic differences (which might well continue to be there at the lower level) became wholly indifferent in relation to the one thing that mattered. That this was possible was due to the fact that external identity markers (circumcision, food laws, etc.) were shorn of their original identity-creating function in favor of a single identity marker that is internal: Christ faith and reception of the pneuma in the hearts.

But also definitely no: where the previous identity markers created boundaries between those on the inside and those on the outside, exactly the same goes for the new identity marker. Either one would be in Christ, with all that this implies (resurrection and life), or one would not (the result being eternal death). Here there is no universalism. Instead, Paul *reinterpreted* his own traditional *ethnos* (namely, Judaism) in such a manner that it became accessible across the traditional ethnic boundaries. But he also *retained* the exclusive character of his new ethnos from the traditional notion of the Jewish ethnos. Paul's new ethnos does contain a universalistic element when compared with traditional ethnic boundaries, one that is precisely due to the *internal* character of the crucial identity marker, but it also contains a strong element of boundary drawing—only, the boundary has now been placed elsewhere than in the conception of the Jewish ethnos from which he started.

The crucial difference from the traditional way of thinking about the world is the following. Up to now, one had been thinking about values on the same level. Either one was a Jew with such and such traditional, clearly observable ethnic identity markers or one was a non-Jew with such and such identity markers. Against this, Paul managed to articulate his own position by means of a way of thinking that had a *double* character: unity at one level—*but also the possibility of a plurality at a different, subordinate level.* As we recall, traditional values and identity markers (e.g., Jewish ones) were on the one hand completely irrelevant (with regard to justice and salvation and one's ultimate identity); on the other hand, they might continue to play a role as long as they did not in any way interfere with the only thing that mattered. Non-Jews could (indeed, they *must*) continue to live as non-Jews (though not in relation to their previous gods), and (traditional) Jews might very well continue to live as (traditional) Jews. That was quite all right—at the *subordinate* level. Indeed, of himself (a Jew!), Paul could even say that in *relation* to non-Jews, he lived *as* a non-Jew and in *relation* to Jews, he lived *as* a Jew! *Above* that, there was the Christ gospel, which even *called* him to live exactly like that. (For all this, see 1 Cor 9:19–23, **T2.13**.) It is this double way of thinking concerning values that we must get hold of. It permeates everything Paul says.

This way of thinking shows Paul's true genius, not just of language, but also of thought. Where did he get this idea? Who knows? Still, we already noted that one branch of Greco-Roman philosophy, Stoicism, had developed exactly the same double model in its attempt to understand the relationship between the one thing that is truly good and all the other remaining values that human beings have, like health, wealth, and material goods. The latter were, as the Stoics said and we already know, "indifferent" (Greek *adiaphora*) in relation to happiness. In relation to that, *only* the *true* good mattered (virtue and the like). Nevertheless, the other values might well have a certain significance. For instance, when all things were equal, it was better for a person to be healthy than ill, rich than poor, and so on. (As we noted, the Stoics said that it was "preferable" and "to be taken." It was not *good* but in itself completely indifferent.) If we transfer this to Paul, there was room for differences between Christ believers at a subordinate level: being a Jew or a non-Jew, a master or a slave, a man or a woman. But in relation to what alone mattered at the highest level—being one in Christ—it was completely indifferent whether one was one thing or the other.

Not only was Paul a faith fanatic. He was also a philosopher.

4

THE OPPOSITION

MASTERS AND SLAVES, MEN AND WOMEN, SEX, AND THE REST OF THE WORLD

WE RECALL OUR key verse (Gal 3:26–28):

> (**T0.14**) [26]For in Christ Jesus you are all sons of God through faith. [27]As many of you as were baptized into Christ have clothed yourselves with Christ. [28]There is *no longer Jew or Greek*, there is *no longer slave or free*, there is *no longer male and female*; for *all of you are one in Christ Jesus.*

In the previous chapter, we discussed Jew and Greek. In this chapter, we will consider master and slave and male and female. There are two closely connected main questions: How does Paul apply his basic idea of unity in Christ to groups that continue to display certain social differences? How should we understand the identity of Christ believers once we also consider the social, gender, sexual, and political dimensions of their lives?

MASTERS AND SLAVES

First, on master and slave: In what way "is" there no longer slave or master in Christ? Were Christ-believing slaves meant to be manumitted by their Christ-believing masters? Or were they precisely not meant to be so, which would make their social status literally completely indifferent? It looks as if Paul wanted to say both things.

In the very short letter to Philemon, he is probably arguing for manumission. In 1 Corinthians, he is probably arguing for the status quo and indifference. How was he able to do both?

What this issue is all about is the relationship in Paul's double model between the one thing that is all-important at the highest level (being in Christ) and phenomena at the subordinate level—in this case, that one person is a master (or at least a free person) and another a slave. Does the community in Christ have any direct influence on the social relations at the subordinate level? Or does it not? One would immediately think that it has. For we saw in the case of Christ-believing Jews and non-Jews that the community in Christ did have consequences further down: Jews must no longer ascribe any religious significance to the law of Moses, and non-Jews must no longer ascribe any religious importance to their old gods (the idols!). How, then, in the case of master and slave?

The letter to Philemon has its name from its recipient, Philemon, whom Paul addresses as his "dear friend and co-worker" (Phlm 1). The situation behind the letter is that a slave of Philemon's, Onesimus, has joined Paul, who is imprisoned (probably in Ephesus in western Turkey), without Philemon's permission and knowledge. Paul now sends Onesimus back to Philemon together with the letter itself. In it, Paul employs all his means of persuasion to make Philemon greet Onesimus in the best possible way. But exactly how? The answer is only given implicitly (Phlm 15–16):

> **T4.1** [15]Perhaps this is the reason he was separated from you for a while, so that you might have him back forever, [16]no longer as a slave but more than a slave, a beloved brother—especially to me but how much more to you, both in the flesh and in the Lord.

Of course, a slave might well be a beloved brother. And in Christ, everybody was an equal. But how might Onesimus be a beloved brother *in the flesh* if he was not manumitted? Paul even goes on to say that if Onesimus owes anything to Philemon, Paul will himself pay for it (Phlm 17). It seems obvious that this is all about ransoming Onesimus as something Paul offers to do—if Philemon insists. Thus it is probable that in the letter, Paul is actually asking Philemon to manumit Onesimus so that he may in *all* respects be "a beloved brother."

It is different in 1 Corinthians. In chapter 7, to which we will come back, Paul discusses whether it is OK to marry (or remain married) in the light of the short time that remains before the return of Christ. In principle, Paul's answer is this: status quo! If you are already married, then continue to be so. If you are not, then continue like that. He justifies this position in a text that generalizes the issue and also touches on slavery. The text is central and deserves to be quoted in full (1 Cor 7:17–24):

> **T4.2** [17]However that may be, let each of you lead the life that the Lord has assigned, to which God called you. This is my rule in all the churches. [18]Was anyone at the time of his call already circumcised? Let him not seek to remove the marks of circumcision. Was anyone at the time of his call uncircumcised? Let him not seek circumcision. [19]Circumcision is nothing, and uncircumcision is nothing; but obeying the commandments of God is everything. [20]Let each of you remain in the condition in which you were called. [21]Were you a slave when called? Do not be concerned about it. Even if you can gain your freedom, make use of your present condition now more than ever. [22]For whoever was called in the Lord as a slave is a freed person belonging to the Lord, just as whoever was free when called is a slave of Christ. [23]You were bought with a price; do not become slaves of human masters. [24]In whatever condition you were called, brothers, there remain with God.

In this text, the translation of 7:21 creates difficulties. Should one translate it the way I have done (together with the New Revised

Standard Version [NRSV] in the main text)? Or should one say with the alternative suggestion in NRSV, "(then) avail yourself of the opportunity"? The context as a whole (including 7:22) points in the direction of the former solution. Conversely, we would prefer the apostle to have said what is expressed in the alternative solution. In that case, what he actually meant was probably the former!

Suppose, then, that Paul spoke (even if in a somewhat subdued tone of voice) of manumission in the case of Onesimus and status quo in his more general statement. How was he able to do both? And what does the whole issue tell us about the connection between the relationship among believers within the congregation at the highest level, where they are one in Christ, and their relationship to the outside world at the subordinate level, where there are differences? If masters and slaves were one in Christ and equal within the congregation, were they also equal externally in concrete social practice? Or is the unity in Christ within the congregation only what some people call "spiritual" in such a way that it precisely has no concrete implications for social practice in the world outside the congregation?

When I say "within the congregation," I mean in the *inner* life of the congregation—for instance, during service. This is also a piece of concrete social practice, and from Paul's discussion elsewhere in 1 Corinthians (the second half of chapter 11) of a problem that had arisen in connection with the proper way of celebrating the Eucharist, it is clear that the "spiritual" unity in Christ at least meant equality of social practice in the inner life of the congregation. *All* participants—whether rich or poor—were meant to get an equal share of food during the Eucharist! However, Paul was not a socialist, and he never dreamed of creating equality in society at large. How, then, with the question of slavery? Were slaves meant to be manumitted?

It is probable that Paul's basic view was the one he articulates in 1 Corinthians (**T4.2**). The line between inside and outside the congregation was clear and was not meant to be transcended. As he says in 1 Corinthians 10:32,

> (**T3.7**) [32]Give no offense to Jews or to Greeks or to the church of God.

We also know the justification for this rather passive attitude: "Time has grown short" (1 Cor 7:29, see in **T4.3**); Christ might return at any moment. Paul believed so quite literally. In that case, one would hardly waste many thoughts on seeing the community in Christ enlarged to cover the outside world too. Instead, one is likely to focus as what matters on the community in Christ within the congregation. This whole way of thinking is memorably articulated in chapter 7 of 1 Corinthians when Paul says the following (1 Cor 7:29–31):

> **T4.3** [29]What I mean, brothers, is this: the appointed time has grown short; from now on, let even those who have wives be as if they had none, [30]and those who mourn as if they were not mourning, and those who rejoice as if they were not rejoicing, and those who buy as if they had no possessions, [31]and those who deal with the world as if they had no dealings with it. For the form of this world is passing away.

Dear me! How may one have a wife as if one did not? How may one in general deal with the world as if one had no dealings whatsoever with it? The answer is this: if there is only one thing that genuinely matters—namely, the community in Christ—and if, as a consequence of this, everything else is literally indifferent. That was what Paul thought, and precisely *because* the time was short. We on our side cannot in any way think the same. For it turned out that the time was *not* short. However, *if* one had that belief, it almost goes without saying that the question of a person's social status in society at large (slave or not) was of no importance whatsoever.

In the letter to Philemon, by contrast, what we see is a very careful *attempt* on Paul's part to let the inner community of love within the congregation be extended to one specific person (the slave, Onesimus) in relation to one other specific person (his master, Philemon) also externally in concrete social practice—that is, when they are not interacting together within the inner life of the congregation. It is as if he may have thought this: since they are both Christ believers, *these two* people may well extend the inner community of love within the congregation into concrete social practice outside the congregation.

In these two examples of Paul's way of handling the issue of slavery, we see how he employs in practice his double way of thinking about value. The uppermost value of community in love, which is expressed in Paul's maxim (*Always* think of the good of others, *never* of your own), is the one that reigns in the inner life of the congregation. Here every slave is also concretely a freed person belonging to the Lord (as in **T4.2**), just as whoever is socially free is also a slave—namely, of Christ. This is something that both must and will show itself in social practice within the congregation. In comparison with that, it is completely immaterial—since the time is short—whether a person is a slave or free in society outside the congregation. *Nevertheless*, the latter issue is no more immaterial than that Paul could apparently (even if only somewhat tentatively) exhort one Christ-believing master, Philemon, to extend the equality that he had with his slave within the congregation to hold also outside it—and hence to manumit him. On the one hand, the issue of slavery is *completely* unimportant in relation to the one thing that matters: the Christ faith and the way this shows itself within the congregation. On the other hand, the same issue is not completely unimportant after all. And so one might attempt to handle it in the light of the higher value.

How should we understand the identity of a Christ believer if the person is also socially a slave? The immediate answer would be that this person is a Christ-believing slave. *However*, since the slave's status as a slave is completely unimportant in comparison with what he first and foremost is (namely, one in Christ with all other Christ believers), a better answer is that this person is a Christ believer—who also happens externally to be a slave. To bring out the crucial role of the former half of this, Paul plays his trump card by declaring that the Christ-believing slave is also a *freed* person belonging to the Lord. In Christ (i.e., within the congregation), he is one with all other Christ believers—that is, *not* subordinated to them but their *equal.*

MEN AND WOMEN

Paul was not a feminist. He shared the view of women and men of his own time, and his view may even have been somewhat colored by his own traditional Jewish background. He is famous for having said that "women should be silent in the churches" (1 Cor 14:34–35):

> **T4.4** [34]For they are not permitted to speak, but should be subordinate, as the law also says. [35]If there is anything they desire to know, let them ask their husbands at home. For it is shameful for a woman to speak in church.

These are clear words that have had a huge—and hugely deplorable—impact for two thousand years. But is it Paul himself speaking? Two facts suggest otherwise. The first is that the transmission of these verses in the manuscripts is not wholly secure. They therefore may have been added by some later adherents of Paul who felt the need to put women in their place. The other is that—at least, superficially—the two verses clash with something Paul has said two chapters earlier in the same letter (1 Cor 11:2–16), where he is discussing what kind of head covering women must carry *when* they prophesy in the congregation during service. How would they be able to do the latter if they also were to "be silent in the churches"?

We will look at chapter 11 in a moment. What needs to be said here is that even if Paul himself is not the author of **T4.4**, he might well have been! Paul, as we said, was not a feminist. And it *may* be that **T4.4** in chapter 14 is speaking of something other than chapter 11.

Let us suppose, therefore, that Paul in principle adopted the view of women of his own time. They were not equal with men, and they ought to behave in public life in accordance with this. That is one reason too why all of Paul's letters are in principle addressed to the men in the congregations. When he addresses them as "brothers," the women may well be included. But the focus is on the men. The women only belong at a lower level. If that is how Paul understood it, we must say that he did *not* see the Christ-believing women in the light of his basic idea of unity and equality in Christ. In that case, we must conclude that on this important matter, he let himself be governed as much by a traditional Jewish understanding as by the potential that was perhaps contained in his basic Christ-believing idea. This point is quite central if one considers the role of the relationship between the genders in contemporary Islam—and up through the ages in Christianity.

That only makes Paul's argumentation in chapter 11 of 1 Corinthians all the more striking. The text discusses the issue of head covering during service. To begin with, the following holds (1 Cor 11:4–5):

> **T4.5** [4]Any man who prays or prophesies with something on his head disgraces his head, [5]but any woman who prays or prophesies with her head unveiled disgraces her head.

Paul goes immediately on to justify this—and in a highly Jewish manner (11:3, 7–9):

> **T4.6** [3]But I want you to understand that Christ is the head of every man, and the husband is the head of his wife, and God is the head

> of Christ. . . . [7]For a man ought not to have his head veiled, since he is the image and reflection of God; but woman is the reflection of man. [8]Indeed, man was not made from woman, but woman from man. [9]Neither was man created for the sake of woman, but woman for the sake of man.

Here Paul really brings out the big guns: creation itself as described in Genesis. If nothing else, then this must convince the women: no prayer or prophecy without head covering!

However, things are not quite so simple as that. Once he has referred to the story of creation, the apostle *breaks off* and continues talking of the relationship between men and women *in the Lord*, which means in Christ and hence within the congregation (11:11–12):

> **T4.7** [11]*Nevertheless*, in the Lord woman is not independent of man or man independent of woman. [12]For just as woman came from man, so man comes through woman; but all things come from God.

Thus in Christ, there is actually equality between man and woman. Here there is *not* the subordination that Paul has just described in **T4.6**! What does this mean for the issue of head covering? Paul continues like this (11:13–15):

> **T4.8** [13]*Judge for yourselves*: Is it proper for a woman to pray to God with her head unveiled? [14]Does not nature itself teach you that if a man wears long hair, it is degrading to him, [15]but if a woman has long hair, it is her glory? For her hair is given to her for a covering.

Strange things happen here. First, Paul now appeals to the Corinthians themselves. Second, he appeals to "nature"—or as we would say, to ordinary social practice. Here we are very far from the order of creation. Behind this change in the argumentation lies the fact that Paul now remembers that he is himself speaking as one Christ believer to other Christ believers. As part of this community, he cannot just enforce his own religiously based understanding (creation!). He has both to appeal to the understanding of his addressees on their own and also to introduce a new argument (in his reference to "nature")—an argument to which we on our side cannot ascribe the same importance as Paul apparently did. What we see here is that Paul lets his own maxim and the principle of community in love color and gain the upper hand in his own way of arguing. He continues to believe that the women must pray and prophesy with their heads covered, but he appeals to his addressees to see and understand it for themselves. This strong movement toward consideration for the others is continued in the final verse of the text (11:16):

> **T4.9** [16]But if anyone is disposed to be contentious—we have no such custom, nor do the churches of God.

In other words, if you don't agree, then do as you wish!

This whole text is a striking example of the way in which Paul feels bound by the content of his own message even in his way of arguing. The basic Christ-believing idea of unity in Christ wins out against his inherited and—as he himself thinks—better understanding of the relationship between the genders within the congregation. He believes what he believes about the proper behavior of the women during service. But he ends up avoiding imposing his own view by authoritarian force and instead letting the question be up to the people themselves. Here, too, we see how Paul makes use of his double way of thinking concerning values. The uppermost value suggests one specific way of arguing. If it clashes with a certain understanding of certain subordinate values in concrete social practice, then the uppermost value wins out. In service, so Paul felt, women and men *ought* to behave differently. But if this is prevented by the necessary consideration for others, then one will have to yield.

How, then, should we understand the identity of a Christ believer if the person is also a woman? The immediate answer is this: a Christ-believing woman. Paul in principle sticks to that answer. However, his own message (the central idea of unity in Christ) forces him also—at least tentatively—to give a different answer: a Christ believer—who also happens to be a woman. We have seen in **T4.5–4.9** how Paul operates creatively with his central idea in such a way that it—at least tentatively—changes something as central as the relationship between the genders (but definitely only within the congregation).

SEX

Exactly the same pattern may be found in the famous chapter 7 of 1 Corinthians, which treats sex within marriage and the question of whether one should marry at all. The framing is clear, as we know: "Time has grown short" (1 Cor 7:29); Christ may return any moment (see in **T4.3**). Seen in this light, shouldn't one abstain from sex even if one is married? Or should one in fact marry at all? The Corinthians have disagreed about these two questions, and Paul needs to sort out the threads.

As so often, his answer is a double one. On the one hand, there is of course only one thing that genuinely matters: Christ. We saw that in the famous text **T4.3** (1 Cor 7:29–31). Christ believers must basically live in the world (i.e., outside the congregation) as if they do not do so at all. For only one thing matters: Christ.

Nevertheless, there is also the other side of the issue. First, on sex in marriage. True, it is "well for a man not to touch a woman" (1 Cor 7:1). *But* (7:2–7)

> **T4.10** [2]because of cases of sexual immorality, each man should have his own wife and each woman her own husband. [3]The husband should give to his wife her conjugal rights, and *likewise* the wife to her husband. [4]For the wife does not have authority over

> her own body, but the husband does; *likewise* the husband does not have authority over his own body, but the wife does. [5]Do not deprive one another except perhaps by agreement for a set time, to devote yourselves to prayer, and then come together again, so that Satan may not tempt you because of your lack of self-control. [6]This I say by way of concession, not of command. [7]*I wish that all were as I myself am. But* each has a particular gift from God, one having one kind and another a different kind.

The text almost speaks for itself. But we may note that Paul here puts husband and wife on wholly equal terms. We may also note that he very clearly retains his double way of thinking on the values. The best thing would be that all human beings were like Paul himself on this matter: sexually abstinent (asceticism). That would reflect the fact that time has grown short and that the form of this world is passing away. But Paul's own maxim tells him to make an allowance for the Corinthians, which he then does—and explicitly as an allowance. In this way, too, they will avoid the possibility that Satan in the form of their own lack of self-control may tempt them to what is even worse: apostasy.

Later in the chapter, Paul employs the same double argument in connection with the question whether one should marry at all. On the one hand, he speaks for not marrying (7:32–35):

> **T4.11** [32]I want you to be free from anxieties. The unmarried man is anxious about the affairs of the Lord, how to please the Lord; [33]but the married man is anxious about the affairs of the world, how to please his wife, [34]and his interests are divided. And the unmarried woman and the virgin are anxious about the affairs of the Lord, so that they may be holy in body and pneuma; but the married woman is anxious about the affairs of the world, how to please her husband. [35]I say this for your own benefit, not to put any restraint upon you, but to promote good order and unhindered devotion to the Lord.

This makes immediate sense, and it shows the radical character of Paul's understanding of Christ faith. But then on the other side, there is the sexual urge, which makes its demands. If it does, then it is OK; if not, even better (7:38)! Even though Paul has enjoined in **T4.3** that one must deal with the world as if one had no dealings with it, he nevertheless allows that one does deal with the world with respect to having sex and to marrying in the first place. One may only guess what this kind of sex ("as if not" in **T4.3**—that is, as if one did *not* have it!) may have looked like. The desire itself for sex is one that Paul will hardly have accepted. As a matter of fact, he says in his very first letter (to the Thessalonians) that they must each (1 Thess 4:4–5, see in **T1.10**)

> (**T1.10**) [4]take a wife for himself in holiness and honor, [5]not with lustful passion, like the pagans who do not know God.

The apostle was no warm supporter of sex.

What we find here is once again Paul's quite refined use of his own central idea. Focus must be on Christ, and this would mean abstinence were it not for the fact that the same focus *also* meant the consideration for others (here the addressees of the letter) that constitutes the core of Paul's maxim. Thus Paul's own focus on Christ *forces* him to yield to the needs of the others. With regard to their identity, he must have thought that those Christ believers who in spite of the fact that time had grown short did marry and have sex would have done so "as if not" (see again in **T4.3**) and that their focus on Christ would not therefore be radically disturbed. Otherwise, they might make a temporary pause in order to obtain time for prayer (see 7:5 in **T4.10**). Primarily, then, they are Christ believers—who also happen to be married and so on.

The apostle was even more critical toward homosexual practice. In a notoriously famous passage in chapter 1 of Romans, he uses homosexual practice as an example of the distorted relationship with God that he (as a Jew) in general found among non-Jews. Here is first his description of that relationship (Rom 1:18–23):

> **T4.12** [18]For the wrath of God is revealed from heaven against all ungodliness and wickedness of those who by their wickedness suppress the truth. [19]For what can be known about God is plain to them, because God has shown it to them. [20]Ever since the creation of the world his eternal power and divine nature, invisible though they are, have been understood and seen through the things he has made. So they are without excuse; [21]for though they knew God, they did not honor him as God or give thanks to him, but they became futile in their thinking, and their senseless minds were darkened. [22]Claiming to be wise, they became fools; [23]and they exchanged the glory of the immortal God for images resembling a mortal human being or birds or four-footed animals or reptiles.

Here both Egyptian and Greco-Roman gods are punched in the best Jewish manner. None of Paul's fellow Jews might have said it better. Note also the main point, which is that in their gods, pagans only worship themselves or something even lower. It is this idea that Paul next uses in his account of the punishment that God has given them (1:24, 26–27):

> **T4.13** [24]Therefore, God gave them up in the lusts of their hearts to impurity, to the degrading of their bodies among themselves. . . . [26]For this reason God gave them up to degrading passions. Their women exchanged natural intercourse for unnatural, [27]and in the same way also the men, giving up natural intercourse with women, were consumed with passion for one another. Men committed shameless acts with men and received in their own persons the due penalty for their error.

Dear me! What use has not been made of this text in connection with the HIV epidemic?!

As regards homosexual practice, Paul was as Jewish as anybody. But it is worth adding that behind it all, there is a deeper idea. Paul's point is that homosexual practice, which is directed toward a person of the same gender, is particularly suitable for showing what according to Paul was wrong quite generally with the relationship of non-Jews with God: that it was in fact directed toward themselves. What Paul is after is *self-directedness.* We must insist that he misunderstands homosexuality. It is difficult to see that homosexual practice should be any more self-directed than heterosexual practice. Both are (I suppose) both self-directed and other-directed when they are at their best. Nevertheless, it is only fair to the apostle to point out that his target is not so much homosexual practice in itself as the kind of self-directedness that he (wrongly) finds reflected in homosexual practice.

That this is so is shown by his third and final account of the kind of punishment to which God gave over the pagans in return for their failing acknowledgment of God himself (1:28–32):

> T4.14 28And since they did not see fit to acknowledge God, God gave them up to a debased mind and to things that should not be done.
> 29They were filled with every kind of wickedness, evil, covetousness, malice. Full of envy, murder, strife, deceit, craftiness, they are gossips,
> 30slanderers, God-haters, insolent, haughty, boastful, inventors of evil, rebellious toward parents, 31foolish, faithless, heartless, ruthless.
> 32They know God's decree, that those who practice such things deserve to die—yet they not only do them but even applaud others who practice them.

All the items in the long list of bad things that Paul produces here are characterized by being self-directed. Note in that connection the extra twist that he gives it all toward the end. The ethical punishment that the non-Jews receive for their sinfulness goes so far that they not only themselves commit all these horrible things in their own self-directedness: they also positively *applaud others* when *they* do the same things. Thus they are self-directed precisely when they are other-directed. In truth, a climax of perversion!

We should conclude that although Paul was strongly against homosexual practice (along traditional Jewish lines), he primarily employed this practice (wrongly) as an example of something much more general: self-directedness. The ethics of non-Jews, which reflected their failed theology, was diametrically opposite, Paul thought, of the one that is expressed in his maxim and in the idea of a community in love.

How, then, does Paul himself employ his central idea of community in love? The sad answer is this: as ammunition against a description of homosexual practice that we, on our side, must deem false. Where in relation to women and sex in marriage we found *some* degree of openness on Paul's part in the light of his central idea, we must conclude that his negative attitude toward homosexual practice was so strong that it did not allow for any softening but rather made him use his central idea as ammunition *against* it. Based on his idea of openness toward others, Paul thought that he could expose homosexual practice as *the opposite*: intrinsically an expression of self-directedness.

Once more, we see how central issues of gender are in the development of a religion.

THIS WORLD'S RULERS

Romans contains one more notoriously famous passage that now concerns the relationship of Christ believers to the political rulers. To begin with, the text looks deeply problematic (Rom 13:1–7):

> **T4.15** [1]Let every person be subject to the governing authorities; for there is no authority except from God, and those authorities that exist have been instituted by God. [2]Therefore, whoever resists authority resists what God has appointed, and those who resist will

> incur judgment. [3]For rulers are not a terror to good conduct, but to bad. Do you wish to have no fear of the authority? Then do what is good, and you will receive its approval; [4]for it is God's servant for your good. But if you do what is wrong, you should be afraid, for the authority does not bear the sword in vain! It is the servant of God to execute wrath on the wrongdoer. [5]Therefore, one must be subject, not only because of wrath but also because of conscience. [6]For the same reason you also pay taxes, for the authorities are God's servants, busy with this very thing. [7]Pay to all what is due them—taxes to whom taxes are due, revenue to whom revenue is due, fear to whom fear is due, honor to whom honor is due.

Again, dear me! Not only are there authorities outside the congregation to whom one must submit: those authorities are also the extended arm of God himself! If, as may be the case, Romans was written in the year 54, when Nero had just been installed as emperor, one might perhaps understand this, for at his accession, he was celebrated almost as a liberator. But what would Paul have said ten years later? Moreover, in spite of everything we have seen so far, did Paul not see any divide whatsoever between inside the congregation and outside?

Definitely yes. Here it is important to see that chapter 13 of Romans coheres closely with the immediately preceding chapter 12. There Paul begins by focusing on the ethics inside the congregation, which should be infused with love (12:9). Gradually, however (from 12:14 onward), he extends this attitude to believers' relationship with people outside the congregation. Believers must not "repay anyone evil for evil" but take thought for what is noble in their relations with *all* people (12:17). Indeed, they must not "be overcome by evil" but "overcome evil with good" (12:21)! In all this, there is a very clear sense of the distinction between inside and outside the congregation. An *inside* attitude is being *extended*—in ways that clearly mark a distance—to outside people.

In fact, **T4.15** itself contains two ideas that point in the direction of the same distinction between inside and outside. The first is the justification Paul gives in 13:5: not just in order to escape from fear of the anger of the authorities and of God but also because of one's conscience. In other words, one must also submit to the good and do it *just because* it is good and because one basically wants it oneself. (That is what one's conscience tells one.) The other idea forms part of 13:7: fear the one to whom fear is due (that is presumably precisely the earthly authorities), but honor the one to whom honor is due (that is more likely to be God). Already here, we see the beginning of a distinction of the earthly authorities from God. In short, this whole text is hardly *just* about "submitting to the authorities."

The same movement can be found in the remainder of chapter 13. This shows that **T4.15** must never be read on its own and out of context, where the context is both what precedes and what follows. Paul immediately continues like this (13:8–10):

> (**T2.4**) 8Owe no one anything, except to love one another; for the one who loves another has fulfilled the law. 9The commandments, "You shall not commit adultery; You shall not murder; You shall not steal; You shall not covet"; and any other commandment, are summed up in this word, "Love your neighbor as yourself." 10Love does no wrong to a neighbor; therefore, love is the fulfilling of the law.

In this text, Paul speaks not at all of earthly authorities but of something quite different: of the relationship of Christ believers to the law of Moses. The point is that the law is actually superfluous for them, for in having Christ faith and the love that goes with that (recall Gal 5:6, **T2.1**), they *already* fulfill the law. Note then the transition from **T4.15** into **T2.4** (just quoted): Romans 13:7 says, "Give to all what you owe them," and 13:8 says, "Owe nothing to anybody—other than loving one another." Here Paul is claiming that the Christ believers must, as it were, finish with their ordinary, earthly obligations in such a way that they may then focus *alone* on their obligation as believers to love one another. In this way, it will *also* be the case that they fulfill the law of Moses. We may summarize as follows what Paul is saying in both texts: with regard to both the Roman political authorities and the Jewish legal authority (the law), Christ believers *in advance* fulfill the demands of either when they do what God wants them to do.

In spite of this, is it not also the case that in **T4.15** and **T2.4** (but particularly strongly in **T4.15**), Paul subjects the Christ believers under demands from either political or legal authorities that do not fall under the Christ faith? If anybody were to suspect that, Paul himself in advance rejects it when in the third and final text of the chapter, he says the following (13:11–14):

> (**T0.8**) [11]Besides this, you know what time it is, how it is now the moment for you to wake from sleep. For salvation is nearer to us now than when we became believers; [12]the night is far gone, the day is near. Let us then lay aside the works of darkness and put on the armor of light; [13]let us live honorably as in the day, not in reveling and drunkenness, not in debauchery and licentiousness, not in quarreling and jealousy. [14]Instead, put on the Lord Jesus Christ, and make no provision for the flesh, to gratify its desires.

In this text, Paul places all concretely lived life under the perspective that the return of the Lord is imminent. That is the only thing that matters. Seen in that light, everything else becomes indifferent.

Thus one may summarize the whole of Romans 13 by speaking of a movement *from* being obedient to the Roman political authorities (including by paying one's taxes!) *via* living in love within the congregation (and in this way *fulfilling* the Jewish law of Moses) *to* living with a focus on the imminent return of Christ. It is the last part of this that really matters with regard to the future.

The second to last part is what is important right now. And the first part is in principle indifferent. Once again, we see how Paul's double way of thinking about values structures what he has to say—and here of the external relations of the Christ-believing congregation: both to the Roman political authority and to the Jewish legal authority.

How, then, should we understand the identity of the Christ believers to whom Paul is here writing? The answer must again be this: they are Christ believers (and hence the real Jews, as we know)—who happen to live under Roman administration. With regard to the latter, they do what they must, but only in an external way. In themselves, they are wholly directed elsewhere: toward their imminent salvation.

* * *

How did Paul become able to handle his double way of thinking about values in the richly differentiated way we have seen in this and the previous chapter with regard to the relationship between Jews and non-Jews, masters and slaves, men, women, and sex, and in relation to the political and legal authorities outside the congregation itself? What is the idea that allows him to combine his own personal agenda with all the questions of concrete social practice that are raised by the fact that human beings live in this earthly world?

The answer is that Paul maintained the central perspective of his double way of thinking the whole way through: there is only one thing that matters, and that is the resurrection in the future and the life in the present that directly reflects the resurrection. When he looked at the concrete, earthly living of human beings in that light, he saw that there was room for various types of differentiation concerning that living—those we have seen him develop. Put differently, the fact that a range of ordinary, earthly phenomena were in themselves indifferent when seen in the light of the central perspective allowed him to handle them in a differentiated manner that reflected the fact that the central perspective itself included Paul's own maxim concerning the relationship with others. For this reason, Jews might (if they wanted to) go on living as Jews. Slaves might be manumitted but did not have to be. Women might (if they wanted to) behave like the men (i.e., without a head covering) during service. Married people might have sex—and ought to if they were unable to control the sexual urge. Men and women might marry if it was necessary. Finally, Christ believers both could and should pay their taxes and subject themselves to the political authorities. All of this was to be seen in the light of the fact that these various ways of dealing with the world were in themselves wholly indifferent in comparison with the one thing that mattered: the directedness toward Christ and his immediate return.

It is the combination of a total directedness toward Christ and the specific content of this directedness in Paul's maxim that allows for a fine-grained *differentiation* in the handling of social differences. It is difficult not to feel that this whole way of thinking bears witness to a sharp philosophical mind.

ACTUALIZATION

Just as we cannot immediately make Paul's theology our own, so it is with his ethics. We cannot believe that Christ was imminently about to return and initiate the resurrection of human beings on the day of judgment. For it did not in fact happen in the way Paul had imagined it. Nor can we accept the dislocation of the focus in ethics that followed from Paul's exclusive theological focus. Put differently, we cannot consider all those things indifferent that Paul considered to be so. We cannot accept slavery and have therefore abolished it in our societies. We cannot accept inequality between women and men and have therefore—at least in principle—abolished it in our societies. We cannot accept Paul's view of sex in marriage as a makeshift solution intended to avoid that Satan gets control. We cannot accept his view of homosexual practice. And we cannot accept what is in fact a strongly distancing view of society as such. Basically, we cannot accept his negative view of the flesh and the body and of the social practices in which our bodies are engaged.

And yet! Paul distinguished sharply between two worlds. On the one side, there was the resurrection life in heaven and its anticipation in the present within the congregation. On the other, there was the world outside the congregation. That is one more distinction that we cannot accept. We must think directly *of* the world also when we are thinking of Christ. But once that has been said, there is much more to be gained from Paul also in connection with the ethical themes that we have discussed in this chapter. In the modern world, we have abolished slavery and introduced equality between women and men as an *effect* of the single value for which Paul spoke in its ethical form—community in love, where love is expressed in Paul's maxim: Always think of the good of others, never of your own. This principle gives a right to *the others*—a right that is then also (as seen from the other side) one's own. It creates *equality* between *all*. The moment we extend it to cover society as a whole, it results in equality also wholly concretely in social practice. Thus we have changed our view of homosexual practice as an effect of the same value, which does not allow for discrimination based on the views of the majority. Finally, the introduction of democracy into society is an effect of the same value. All individuals must have their own ideas about how society should be organized and must be free to articulate them and work for them. This, then, pertains also to oneself inasmuch as one recognizes the same right in others.

We should conclude that just as we cannot immediately make Paul's theology our own, so we cannot either with his ethics. Still, we are eminently able to let ourselves be inspired by two things in his ethical thinking: the content of his basic ethical principle of human community in love as expressed in his maxim and the form in which this principle may be applied to particular ethical situations in which we find ourselves. If human community in love is the goal, then Paul's maxim is the rule that we may concretely apply on our way toward that goal.

5

THE PERSUASION

INTEGRATION

WE ALREADY KNOW that the seven genuine Pauline letters are basically occasional interventions, snapshots caused by problems and opposition in Paul's congregations of which he has been informed. Thus the letters are exhortations and encouragements telling the congregations how to solve in concrete practice the conflicts that had arisen. However, Paul also constantly attempted to solve those conflicts in the light of his overall theology: the idea of Jesus's death and resurrection and of its direct relevance for Christ believers both in the future and in the present. What is more, the longer time passed, the longer the letters also became, thereby including also Paul's overall justifications of why the congregations should live as they should. In this way, the letters also gradually became something other than just occasional interventions.

Did he reach his goal? Did he manage to persuade his addressees? Were they convinced? We do not know the answer. At some point, people in the early Christian movement must have been so struck by the letters' persuasiveness and power that they decided to collect them and eventually to incorporate them into the New Testament canon. Through that operation, the letters changed their character from being primarily occasional interventions to becoming authoritative, general statements made by the special figure who the apostle Paul had eventually become within the early Christian movement. Paul had himself laid the foundation for this development in the overall justifications he gave for his individual exhortations.

However, this development did not come about in peace and quiet. We already noticed in the introduction that, as Paul himself bears witness, some of his opponents in Corinth described him as follows (2 Cor 10:10):

> (**T0.5**) [10]For they say, "His letters are weighty and strong, but his bodily presence is weak, and his speech contemptible."

When Paul himself had died, people also found fault with his letters. In the so-called Second Letter of Peter, which is also included in the New Testament, the unknown author at one point appeals to Paul in support of one of his claims (2 Pet 3:15). But he also adds this (3:16):

> **T5.1** [16]. . . speaking of this as he does in all his letters. There are some things in them hard to understand, which the ignorant and unstable twist to their own destruction, as they do the other Scriptures.

Thus Paul was anything but uncontroversial in his own time or immediately after.

Even though we do not know the effect of the letters on their immediate addressees, and even though their content was contested when it had been torn away from the particular situations to which they had responded, it is worth asking about their rhetoric. How did Paul *attempt* to convince his readers, thereby making them live the way he recommends? What does he do with his language in order to reach this goal? We will see that one thing he does is bring himself centrally into the act of persuasion. That motif has two sides to it. It partly has an integrative function: Paul and his addressees belong together. But it also has a disintegrative function. Here Paul creates divisions between the addressees and himself. After all, he is their apostle, directly sent out by God, and so on. In addition, Paul may also create sharp divisions between himself and his direct opponents. Both when he works to integrate and to disintegrate, Paul's speaking of himself serves a rhetorical function, which is to convince his addressees. However, when he refers to himself for disintegrative purposes, we also get closer to his own person—or at least to the *persona* that he creates of himself in the letters. We will come back to that in the next chapter, where we will attempt to obtain a full picture of Paul. Until then, we will focus on other sides of his writing, including those that bring Paul himself in for integrative purposes.

What is our own purpose with all this? Answer: to clarify the connection one may find in Paul between the content of his message and the form through which he communicates it. It is this connection we are after. If there is something central in the content itself that we may use (while also neglecting substantial parts of it, as we have seen), and if there is an intrinsic connection between the content and the manner in which it is communicated, then we must also study the latter. For then there might also be something in the form of communication itself that we may ourselves use. Thus where we have hitherto been discussing certain particular themes in the letters, we now turn to their communicative level as a whole. But we do it for a specific purpose, which presupposes the earlier thematic discussion. We now want to see whether there is a match between the content (the themes) and the form in which it is presented, a match that we might ourselves use.

PAUL—AND HIS CO-WORKERS

Paul's letters are in fact not just Paul's. Normally, his letters mention several senders to begin with. Here is the introduction to the earliest letter, 1 Thessalonians (1:1):

> **T5.2** [1][A] Paul, Silvanus, and Timothy, [B] to the church of the Thessalonians in God the Father and the Lord Jesus Christ: [C] Grace to you and peace.

I have added the letters A–C to mark the basic structure of the Pauline letter greeting. We will see that it is repeated again and again. Gradually, however, it also becomes markedly extended, which is interesting in itself. In the present context, the point is that Paul includes a mention of Silvanus and Timothy. We are meant to understand that the letter is sent not only by Paul but by the whole group of workers in Christ whose spokesman Paul is. We may also guess that the Thessalonians already knew both Silvanus and Timothy. Thus it is clear that this practice had a highly integrative function. It is not just Paul speaking but the whole group of Christ believers behind the letter, whom they already know: How, then, will the recipients of the letter react on their side? Will they meet the group of senders and agree with them? Or will they react by maintaining a division? Thus the immediate rhetorical agenda of the letter is to generate agreement in the group. We may connect this with Paul's overall agenda, which lies in generating a genuine community, the community of love that follows from faith in Jesus's death and resurrection. Here, then, there is a close match between the rhetorical practice in the letter and Paul's overall agenda.

Other letters make use of the same pattern. Take, for instance, 1 Corinthians, which is somewhat later. Here Paul at least includes one co-worker, Sosthenes (of whom we know nothing). But Paul's own role and status are emphasized, and the same holds of the addressees themselves, the Corinthians (1 Cor 1:1–3):

> **T5.3** [1][A] Paul, called to be an apostle of Christ Jesus by the will of God, *and our brother Sosthenes*, [2][B] to the church of God that is in Corinth, to those who are sanctified in Christ Jesus, called to be saints, °together with all those who in every place call on

> the name of our Lord Jesus Christ, both their Lord and ours\: [3][C] Grace to you and peace from God our Father and the Lord Jesus Christ.

Note here the words that stand between ° and \. It is probable that they have been added in later manuscripts, bearing witness to the later process of generalization that the Pauline letters have undergone. Apart from that, one finds the same basic form of the greeting with more senders than one as in 1 Thessalonians—but also with an intensified presentation of both Paul himself and the addressees.

Compare this with the beginning of 2 Corinthians, where the self-presentation is a bit more formulaic and the presentation of the Corinthians lacks the earlier warmth. Still, here, too, Paul mentions one co-worker, Timothy (2 Cor 1:1–2):

> **T5.4** [1][A] Paul, an apostle of Christ Jesus by the will of God, *and Timothy our brother*, [B] to the church of God that is in Corinth, *including all the saints throughout Achaia*: [2][C] Grace to you and peace from God our Father and the Lord Jesus Christ.

Here, too, there is an expansion of the recipients of the letter greeting so as not just to be the congregation in Corinth. But here the expansion is no doubt original. Just as Paul creates a broader, integrative basis for his message to the Corinthians by including Timothy among the senders, so he does the same by including among the recipients other Christ believers *in the Corinthians' own neighborhood* in the region of Achaia, to which Corinth itself belonged. In this way, what Paul aims to say to the Corinthians is turned into something bigger. They must understand that their specific response does not just concern themselves. There is a whole group standing on the other side. How, then, will they themselves respond to them? Are they in favor or not?

Thus Paul in principle wishes to include some co-workers in his letter greetings. The purpose is clearly integrative. All the more striking is the letter greeting in two other letters: Galatians and Romans. Here first is Galatians (Gal 1:1–5):

> **T5.5** [1][A] Paul an apostle—sent neither by human commission nor from human authorities, but through Jesus Christ and God the Father, who raised him from the dead—[2]*and all the brothers who are with me,* [B] to the churches of Galatia: [3][C] Grace to you and peace from God our Father and the Lord Jesus Christ, [4]who gave himself for our sins to set us free from the present evil age, according to the will of our God and Father, [5]to whom be the glory forever and ever. Amen.

In this greeting, Paul enormously expands the presentation of himself, and it is clear already here that no matter what his addressees might say or think, it is Paul who is right! In spite of this, he also includes in 1:2 *all* the Christ-believing brothers around him. The Galatians must not believe that the letter is *only* Paul's! In this case, too, the letter greeting has an integrative function. At the same time, we also see Paul make use of himself in a manner that very clearly distinguishes and separates him from his addressees. Thus this particular text also belongs in the next chapter of this book. In addition, in the letter greeting to the Galatians, Paul also expands the final part of the greeting with a whole verse: 1:4. We have not seen anything similar before. It is clear that Paul here wishes to emphasize what the "grace" and "peace" that go into the final part of the letter greeting are all about: grace and peace from *God* as shown in Christ's fate. The creativity in all this is striking.

Consider then Romans, a letter, as we know, in which Paul is writing to one or more congregations in Rome that he had not himself founded (Rom 1:1–7):

> **T5.6** [1][A] Paul, a servant of Jesus Christ, called to be an apostle, set apart for the gospel of God, [2]which he promised beforehand through his prophets in the holy Scriptures, [3]the gospel concerning his Son, who was descended from David according to the flesh [4]and was determined as Son of God with power according to the pneuma of holiness by resurrection from the dead, Jesus Christ our Lord, [5]through whom we have received grace and apostleship to bring about the obedience of faith among all the gentiles for the sake of his name, [6]including yourselves who are called to belong to Jesus Christ, [7][B] to all God's beloved in Rome, who are called to be saints: [C] Grace to you and peace from God our Father and the Lord Jesus Christ.

This is magnificent, and one might write a commentary to the whole letter by developing what Paul says in these seven verses. He succeeds in doing two quite different things, which he nevertheless manages to combine into a single statement. First, he introduces himself. Second, he explains the essence of the message with which he plans to come to Rome. The connection is established by his claim that it is God himself who has been directly involved in both cases. God has called Paul and appointed him to preach God's own gospel (1:1, 5). And God has been directly active in the various events that form part of this gospel (1:2–4). In fact, the Greek words underlying "set apart" in 1:1 and "determined" in 1:4 consist of two variants of the same verb: to "delimit" or "determine." In other words, God steers everything, including Paul's own appeal to the Romans in this very letter. Since Paul does not mention any co-senders, the letter greeting in this particular letter has no integrative function. And yet! By the way he phrases his address to the Romans in 1:6 ("among whom are also *you*"), Paul in advance integrates his addressees into the great drama of God's own intervention that he has just described. They want to be part of that, don't they?

We should conclude that Paul normally mentions other co-senders in the introduction to his letters, aiming in this way to make the letter a piece of communication between two *groups*, not just more or less authoritatively between the addressees and their apostle. In this way, the letter greeting has an integrative function. There is a larger community that Paul invites his addressees to share in. After all, that kind of community constitutes the whole content of his message. In two letters, however, we have seen that Paul primarily or even exclusively mentions himself. In Galatians, the reason is, as he later says, that he is "perplexed" about them (Gal 4:20, see in **T3.2**). In Romans, he is introducing himself to congregations that he did not know beforehand but planned to visit. Still, here, too, he is doing his utmost to integrate his addressees into a community with himself.

"WE"—AND "I"

We should spend a few words on a way of speaking that lies in direct continuation of Paul's mention of his co-senders: the fact that he in principle writes "we" in the letters, not "I." First Thessalonians is a good example. After the letter greeting (**T5.2**), Paul speaks almost the whole way through as a "we" (1 Thess 1:2–6):

> **T5.7** [2]We always give thanks to God for all of you and mention you in our prayers, constantly [3]remembering before our God and Father your work of faith and labor of love and steadfastness of hope in our Lord Jesus Christ. [4]For we know, brothers beloved by God, that he has chosen you, [5]because our message of the gospel came to you not in word only, but also in power and in the holy pneuma and with full conviction; just as you know what kind of persons we proved to be among you for your sake. [6]And you became imitators of us and of the Lord.

He continues in the same way until he is forced to be more specific (2:17–18):

> **T5.8** [17]As for us, brothers, when, for a short time, we were made orphans by being separated from you—face to face, not in heart—we longed with great eagerness to see you face to face. [18]For we wanted to come to you—*I, Paul, again and again*—but Satan blocked our way.

From "we" to "I" and back again.

The same pattern is found a little later. Paul has spoken of his uncertainty about the steadfastness of the Thessalonians after he left them. He now tells them what he then did (3:1–2, 5):

> **T5.9** [1]Therefore, when *we* could bear it no longer, *we* decided to be left *alone* in Athens; [2]and we sent Timothy, our brother and co-worker for God in proclaiming the gospel of Christ, to strengthen and encourage you for the sake of your faith. . . . [5]For this reason, when *I personally* could bear it no longer, I sent to find out about your faith; I was afraid that somehow the tempter [i.e., Satan] might have tempted you and that our labor had been in vain.

Thus Paul prefers to use the integrative "we," even when he writes "we alone," in spite of the fact that his "we" in, for instance, **T5.7** and **T5.8** no doubt refers primarily to himself. From time to time, however, he is forced to speak specifically about himself ("I personally" in **T5.9**).

Seen in this light, it is even more striking when he does speak of an "I." This theme, too, strictly belongs in our next chapter. For here Paul is normally far from integrative. Nevertheless, for the benefit of the reader, I give some examples already here that show the subtlety of the apostle's use of language.

Consider first the letter to the Galatians, which is very far from being integrative. In Galatians 4:12–20 (**T3.2**), Paul speaks throughout in the first-person singular of his own personal relationship with the Galatians both previously and in the present. In Galatians 6:11, he begins his concluding attack on his opponents—the people who stand behind the Galatians' errors—in the following way:

> **T5.10** [11]See what large letters I make when I am writing in my own hand!

Here, too, the use of the first-person singular serves a specific purpose that is anything but integrative. On the contrary, here the apostle really is writing with "large letters"! This continues in the rest of the letter (Gal 6:14–17, see in **T0.6–7**) until Paul may return, in the very last verse of the letter and with a glimmer of hope, one suspects, to the more integrative "we" (Gal 6:18):

> **T5.11** [18]May the grace of our Lord Jesus Christ be with your pneuma, brothers. Amen.

In Romans, too, Paul in principle employs the first-person singular: "I." After the introductory letter greeting (**T5.6**), the letter continues with a thanksgiving in the singular, in which Paul explains why he is writing to the Romans (1:8–15). He returns to the purpose of the letter toward the end (15:14–33). Here, too, he speaks in the first-person singular. But note the linguistic subtlety. Right here the use of the singular is massively integrative: Paul aims to make the Romans positive toward him before his first visit with them. He begins with what is a clear use of a *captatio benevolentiae*, a rhetorical trick by which a speaker tries to capture his listener's benevolence (15:14):

> **T5.12** [14]I myself feel confident about you, my brothers, that you yourselves are full of goodness, filled with all knowledge, and able to instruct one another.

In other words, we need not have two different parties here. You are already able on your own! Paul even goes immediately on to apologize for the letter as a whole (15:15):

> **T5.13** [15]Nevertheless on some points I have written to you rather boldly by way of reminder, because of the grace given me by God.

If he has been too bold (for they already know it!), this is in any case no more than a reminder. Nevertheless, it is justified, for Paul has received a gift of grace from God. He continues by mentioning what this gift consists in (15:16):

> **T5.14** [16]to be a minister of Christ Jesus to the gentiles in the priestly service of the gospel of God, so that the offering of the gentiles may be acceptable, sanctified by holy pneuma.

In this text, Paul clearly invests his own task with as much holiness as he can. It is true that he has spoken relatively boldly to them, for they already know it themselves. Still, he is fully justified in doing so, for behind him stands God himself. Can he be so sure? Yes, this is how he ends (15:17–19):

> **T5.15** [17]In Christ Jesus, then, I have reason to boast of my work for God. [18]For I will not venture to speak of anything except what *Christ has accomplished through me* to win obedience from the gentiles, by word and deed, [19]by the power of signs and wonders, by the power of the pneuma of God.

Put differently, whatever Paul has done as part of his missionary activity is derived directly from Jesus Christ and the pneuma that Paul has received through him. It is not just God who stands behind Paul: Jesus Christ and the pneuma do so too! We must take it that when Paul speaks in Romans 15:14–19 in the first-person singular, it is certainly not just Paul himself who is addressing the Romans but through him also God in the shape of Jesus Christ and the pneuma.

However, Paul never forgets that his whole agenda is a matter of a "we." That is why he concludes his remarks on the purpose of the letter (15:14–33) in the following way (15:30–33):

> **T5.16** [30]I encourage you, brothers, by our Lord Jesus Christ and by the love of the pneuma, *to fight together with me* in your prayers to God on my behalf, [31]that I may be rescued from the unbelievers in Judea, and that my ministry to Jerusalem [a gift of money] may be acceptable to the saints, [32]so that by God's will I may come to you with joy and relax *in your company.* [33]The God of peace be with all of you. Amen.

In this text, Paul does everything he can to integrate his addressees into his own project. They must fight on his behalf to secure that he be saved—and that he may come to them with joy so that they may relax together. Throughout, the idea is that they and he himself must be one and act in unison. That, too, is the essence of his message itself.

Is this, then, the way he concludes the letter? Not at all! There follows a whole chapter that enlarges the perspective in a striking manner. The letter is not just about Paul (and Christ and God) and its addressees but also about a long list of other Christ believers who are, as it were, coming together with Paul in the letter. He first recommends "our sister Phoebe," who may have actually delivered the letter (16:1–2):

> **T5.17** [1]I commend to you our sister Phoebe, a deacon of the congregation at Cenchreae [near Corinth], [2]so that you may welcome her in the Lord as is fitting for the saints, and help her in

> whatever she may require from you, for she has been a benefactor of many and of myself as well.

This exhortation obviously has an integrative function. When Phoebe turns up with such a recommendation, the Romans *must* respond positively both to her and to the letter. Note also that it is a woman whom Paul is recommending in this way. In spite of the fact that Paul was no feminist (as we saw in chapter 4), he nevertheless acknowledged the facts: women had a more central position in the early Christian movement than normally in society at large.

Next, Paul asks his addressees to give greetings from him to a long list of Christ believers who were apparently present in Rome and whom Paul knew. Mentioned by name are more than twenty-six different people of either gender. And please note, the *Romans* are asked to greet *them* from *Paul*. The desire for integration is very strong here. Even more (16:16), as he concludes,

> **T5.18** [16]Greet one another with a holy kiss. All the congregations of Christ greet you.

It is difficult to find a stronger way of expressing the symbiosis that Paul intends to bring about between all involved, one that directly reflects the whole content of his message.

Paul even ends the letter by bringing specific greetings from the place where he found himself (i.e., Corinth) when he wrote the letter (16:21–23):

> **T5.19** [21]Timothy, my co-worker, greets you; so do Lucius and Jason and Sosipater, my relatives. [22]I Tertius, the writer of this letter, greet you in the Lord. [23]Gaius, who is host to me and to the whole church, greets you. Erastus, the city treasurer [of the city of Corinth], and our brother Quartus, greet you.

What is meant by saying that it is Tertius who has written the letter? Answer: Paul dictated the letter; Tertius literally wrote it—and managed to insert *his own* greeting to the Romans! It is likely that Paul has adopted the same procedure in the other letters—apart from where he states that he has himself written with "large letters" (see in **T5.10**). But by letting Tertius himself speak in the letter, Paul forges a direct bond between the Romans, who now *receive* the letter that Tertius has written, and the group around Paul when he dictated it.

We should conclude that Paul in principle wishes to include his co-workers in the letters by a "we." When he speaks in the first-person singular, there is always some reason that calls for special emphasis. This overall practice reflects the content itself of his whole message.

THANKSGIVING AND PRAISE

After the letter greeting, Paul normally provides a so-called thanksgiving section, in which he thanks God for the good behavior of his addressees when they received his message in the first place. In rhetorical terms, this section also has an integrative function. Who does not like to be thanked for something or even praised for it?

Once more, the style is set in 1 Thessalonians 1:2–5, which we will repeat here:

> **T5.20** [2]We always give thanks to God for all of you and mention you in our prayers, constantly [3]remembering before our God and Father your work of faith and labor of love and steadfastness of hope in our Lord Jesus Christ. [4]For we know, brothers beloved by God, that he has chosen you, [5]because our message of the gospel came to you not in word only, but also in power and in the holy pneuma and with full conviction.

Faith, love, and hope as expressed in practice: that was the response of the Thessalonians when they received the gospel. And Paul now thanks God for that. It is difficult to think of a more efficient type of *captatio benevolentiae*: you are still there, right?

However, Paul needs to be certain. So now they are going to be praised even more. It is noteworthy that this happens through the use of a motif to which we will repeatedly come back: that of *reminding* them of what happened at the time when the message of the gospel came to them. Immediately after **T5.20**, Paul continues like this (1 Thess 1:5–10, repeated from **T0.3**):

> **T5.21** [5](Not in word only, but also in power and in holy pneuma and with full conviction,) just as you know what kind of persons we proved to be among you for your sake. [6]And you became imitators of us and of the Lord, for in spite of persecution you received the word with joy in holy pneuma, [7]so that you became an example to all the believers in Macedonia and in Achaia. [8]For the word of the Lord has sounded forth from you not only in Macedonia and Achaia, but in every place your faith in God has become known, so that we have no need to speak about it. [9]For the people of those regions report about us what kind of welcome we had among you, and how you turned to God from idols, to serve a living and true God, [10]and to wait for his Son from heaven, whom he raised from the dead—Jesus, who rescues us from the wrath that is coming.

Imitation of Paul and (through him) of Christ himself, thereby becoming an example to others: there are several motifs here to which we will come back. For the moment, we are interested in the praise. It is evident that by reminding the Thessalonians of their original behavior and praising them for it, Paul aims to bind them to that behavior. And it is all part of his introductory thanksgiving to God for the same behavior. This theme is so important to Paul that he repeats it a little later in spite of the fact that he has now turned to describing his *own* original behavior (1 Thess 2:1–12). He breaks this off in the following way (2:13):

> **T5.22** [13]We also constantly give thanks to God for this, that when you received the word of God that you heard from us, you accepted it not as a human word but as what it really is, God's word, which is also [presently] at work in you believers.

The last addition in this shows how Paul aims to connect the situation then with the situation now through his thanksgiving and the praise that it contains. The underlying purpose is to create and strengthen the integration that is also his overall theme.

We find another example of this movement in the thanksgiving section of Philippians (1:3–11). Here Paul speaks in the first-person singular even though in the initial greeting, he has mentioned Timothy (1:1). This personal tone runs through the whole letter, which is probably due to the fact that Paul is in prison and writing to the Philippians as his friends. Seen in that light, the purpose of the thanksgiving section is to bind *all* the Philippians to Paul by reminding them of what he calls their sharing or community in the gospel—and praising them for it (1:3–6):

> **T5.23** [3]I thank my God every time I remember you, [4]constantly praying with joy in every one of my prayers for all of you, [5]because of your sharing in the gospel from the first day until now. [6]I am confident of this, that the one [i.e., God] who began a good work among you will bring it to completion by the day of Jesus Christ.

We already know the pattern: Paul himself and God—and then the letter's addressees in a community that was established when they came to faith and must continue to the day of judgment.

The same pattern is also found in 1 Corinthians (1:4–9). That only makes it even more noteworthy when the pattern is broken. In 2 Corinthians, where Paul is much more doubtful about the Corinthians' steadfastness, the thanksgiving section still has the form of a praise of God (1:3–11). But what he is thankful for is definitely not the Corinthians but rather the consolation that God has given Paul in all his misery—a misery that is very much due to the Corinthians themselves. We will return to this text in a moment (**T5.28**).

In Galatians, the thanksgiving section has been replaced by one of astonishment (Gal 1:6–7, see in **T3.1**):

> (**T3.1**) [6]I am astonished that you are so quickly deserting the one [God? Paul himself?] who called you in the grace of Christ and are turning to a different gospel—[7]which does not exist, but there are some who are confusing you and want to pervert the gospel of Christ.

In Romans, however, where Paul is aiming to establish from scratch a community between himself and his addressees that he presupposes in other letters, he is back on track (Rom 1:8–10):

> **T5.24** [8]First, I thank my God through Jesus Christ for all of you, because your faith is proclaimed throughout the world. [9]For God, whom I serve with my pneuma by announcing the gospel of his Son, is my witness that without ceasing I remember you always in my prayers, [10]asking that by God's will I may somehow at last succeed in coming to you.

Paul himself with his God on the one side; his thanks for the addressees on the other side and praise for them for being already where they should be; and then his prayer (to his God) that he, Paul, may *at long last* get to visit them: all of this shows especially clearly that Paul's thanksgiving and praise serve the rhetorical purpose of establishing the community between the apostle and his addressees that he aims to bring about by means of the letter as a whole. But further, that kind of community also constitutes the core of his whole message.

BETWEEN THEN AND NOW

In his thanksgiving sections, Paul regularly goes back to the time when his addressees came to have faith and praises them for it. But he also spends much time on telling them how he has himself related to them in the interim period between his leaving them and the time of writing. The purpose continues to be the same: to bind the two parties as tightly together as possible.

The pattern is clear already in 1 Thessalonians. Once Paul has described his own behavior toward the Thessalonians when he was with them for the first time (2:1–12) and once he has again thanked *them* for *their* behavior at the same time (2:13–16, compare **T5.22**), he goes on to inform them of his own mental state (2:17–18, **T5.8**):

> (**T5.8**) [17]*As for us*, brothers, when, for a short time, *we were made orphans by being separated from you*—face to face, not in heart—*we longed with great eagerness* to see you face to face. [18]For we wanted to come to you—I, Paul, again and again—but Satan blocked our way.

And thus it continues into chapter 3. Paul was so concerned about the Thessalonians that he decided to remain in Athens but to send Timothy to Thessaloniki in order to hear what the situation was like there (3:1–5). Great was his joy when Timothy returned with the report that the situation was just fine (3:6–10). Then Paul is able to conclude this long description of his time *with* them (2:1–12) and the time *after* that (2:17–3:10) with a prayer that he may soon get to see them *again*—and that they, on their side, may grow in love up until the day of judgment (3:11–13):

> **T5.25** [11]Now may our God and Father himself and our Lord Jesus direct our way to you. [12]And may the Lord make you increase and

abound in love for one another and for all, just as we abound in love for you. [13]And may he so strengthen your hearts in holiness that you may be blameless before our God and Father at the coming of our Lord Jesus with all his saints.

In this way, Paul spends the whole first half of his letter to the Thessalonians (chapters 1–3) on thanking and praising them, on reminding them of the time when he was with them, and on telling them of his own attitude toward them in the interim period. This is all aimed at maintaining a sense of community, unity, and agreement between the two parties, one that directly reflects the content of his whole message. When this has been established—and that constitutes the deepest purpose of the letter—Paul may continue (in chapters 4–5) to attend to some particular questions that have bothered the congregation.

The pattern of telling about Paul's own situation in the interim period between then and now is repeated in other letters—for instance, in Philippians, where Paul begins in the following way just after the thanksgiving section (1:12):

T5.26 [12]I want you to know, beloved, that *what has happened to me* has actually helped to spread the gospel.

He goes on to explain this in detail in spite of the fact that what he is able to tell them concerns his being in prison and risking capital punishment. But the end of this section shows that this is all, in fact, relevant to the addressees and to their mutual relationship (1:25–26):

T5.27 [25]Since I am convinced of this, I know that I will remain [on earth and so not die] and continue with all of you for your progress and joy in faith, [26]so that I may share abundantly in your boasting in Christ Jesus when I come to you again.

When Paul writes about his own life between then and now, it is always with a view to (re)create the community between the two parties.

A striking example of Paul's use of the same pattern is to be found in 2 Corinthians. In this letter, in spite of what many scholars have claimed, as many as seven chapters (chapters 1–7) are held tightly together by the use of just this pattern. We already noted that Paul employs the thanksgiving section to recount the afflictions he has himself suffered and the consolation that God has given him (1:3–7). It is worth quoting this text here, since it shows to what extent Paul was prepared to employ his own affliction as a basis for a piece of integration:

> **T5.28** [3]Blessed be the God and Father of our Lord Jesus Christ, the Father of mercies and the God of all consolation, [4]who *consoles us in all our affliction*, so that we may be able to console those who are in any affliction with the consolation with which we ourselves are consoled by God. [5]For just as the sufferings of Christ are abundant for us, so also our consolation is abundant through Christ. [6]If we are being afflicted, it is for *your* consolation and salvation; if we are being consoled, it is for *your* consolation, which you experience when you patiently endure *the same sufferings that we are also suffering.* [7]Our hope for you is unshaken; for we know that as you share in our sufferings, so also you share in our consolation.

Paul and the Corinthians share the afflictions and consolation that are in both cases derived from those suffered by the great archetype, Christ. In addition, when Paul himself is afflicted and consoled, it is always for the sake of the Corinthians. That does not matter to him, however, since he feels certain (!) that they on their side will overcome all afflictions and derive consolation from that. The intensity in all this is great. One wonders how the Corinthians may have reacted to it.

The afflictions Paul mentions in his own case primarily (1:8–11) consisted in an imprisonment in Asia Minor, probably the imprisonment in Ephesus in western Turkey from which Paul also wrote his letter to the Philippians. Gradually, however, it becomes clear that Paul's afflictions are just as much due to his concern for the Corinthians. He asserts his sincerity toward them (1:12–14), and he mentions (1:15–2:13) that he wrote a letter to them (which may well be 1 Cor) but also that once he had escaped from prison, he went north from Ephesus in the direction of northern Greece (Macedonia) in order to get to Corinth by that route. Here he first arrived in Troas in northwestern Turkey, hoping to find there his co-worker Titus, whom he had sent to Corinth to find out about the situation there. But when he did not find Titus in Troas, he immediately crossed over into Macedonia (2 Cor 2:12–13):

> **T5.29** [12]When I came to Troas to proclaim the good news of Christ, a door was opened for me in the Lord; [13]but *my mind could not rest* because I did not find my brother Titus there. So I said farewell to them and went on to Macedonia.

At this point, Paul apparently breaks off his account of his own life between then and now by asserting his own innocence and sincerity in preaching the gospel. This happens in a long section that scholars have traditionally seen as a digression (2:14–7:4)—that is, an inserted text whose theme is different from that of the surrounding texts. To my mind, that is wrong. In reality, the long self-reflection that makes up the so-called digression constitutes the content of Paul's thoughts while he was, as it were, standing on the "ferry" between Turkey (Asia) and Macedonia (Europe). It thus belongs intrinsically to Paul's account of his own life between then and now. At the time, so he now says, he reflected on *how* sincerely and openly he had preached the gospel in a manner that precisely corresponded to the gospel itself. He claims to have done this everywhere—but not least to the Corinthians, to whom this whole section is directed. It all issues in one of the most intense passages he ever wrote, in which he reaches strongly out toward them—but still only in his thought (6:11–13; 7:2–4):

> **T5.30** [6:11]We have spoken frankly to you Corinthians; our heart is wide open to you. [12]There is no restriction in our affections, but only in yours. [13]In return—I speak as to children—open wide your hearts also. . . . [7:2]Make room in your hearts for us; we have wronged no one, we have corrupted no one, we have taken advantage of no one. [3]I do not say this to condemn you, for I said before that you are in our hearts, to die together and to live together. [4]I often boast about you; I have great pride in you; I am filled with consolation; I am overjoyed in all our affliction.

This brings us back to Paul's afflictions, but we now know that they were primarily due to the Corinthians—and also that they had been replaced by consolation *and joy*. How? Well (7:5–7), he says,

> **T5.31** [5]For even when we came into Macedonia, our bodies had no rest, but we *were afflicted in every way*—disputes without and fears within. [6]But God, who consoles the downcast, consoled us by the arrival of Titus, [7]and not only by his coming, but also by the consolation with which he was consoled about you, as he told us of your longing, your mourning, your zeal for me, *so that I rejoiced still more.*

In short, Titus at long last showed up coming from Corinth and being able to report that everything was fine there. The Corinthians were wholly with Paul—and so he was filled with joy. Paul goes on to celebrate this (7:8–16), and he ends like this (7:16):

> **T5.32** [16]*I rejoice*, in that I may have complete confidence in you.

From affliction to joy—the whole development is vividly presented by describing Paul's own life between then and now. In seven long chapters (more than half the whole letter), he has employed this literary artifice in order to reestablish the positive relationship between the two parties that apparently risked getting lost. The core of this procedure is to describe Paul's life in the interim period in relation to his addressees. They were constantly in his thoughts. From his side, there had been a complete openness toward them aimed at maintaining their shared sense of community. He now learned that there was a similar openness from the other side. The result: joy!

Was Paul, then, successful? Was he right to react with sheer joy to the reports given by Titus? Certainly not. For in the rest of the letter, he speaks much more sternly to the Corinthians. More on that in the next chapter. Note also that there was no doubt a reason he spent so much time in his letter on recounting the psychodrama that he underwent in relation to the Corinthians on the "ferry" across the Hellespont (2 Cor 2:14–7:4): he could not *in fact* feel certain about them (in spite of **T5.32**)! This only makes it even more striking that he *begins* the letter (the whole of chapters 1–7) by trying to generate as much integration as he possibly could. For this, the pattern of describing his own relationship to his addressees in the interim period between then and now was eminently suitable. *How* worried he had been! And *how* happy he was when he learned that both parties were fully on the same line! In short, so Paul is saying, the community between them *must* continue. And why? Not just for strategic reasons but because that kind of community is what Paul's message is all about.

THEY ALREADY KNOW IT

Paul employs one more rhetorical trick to maintain the community with his addressees that it is his ultimate purpose to establish. He again and again appeals to their own understanding: they already know it all! The idea is that they already find themselves where Paul (also) wishes them to be—and of course as having been *brought* there by Paul himself when he was with them for the first time. Since they already know it, Paul's only task now is to remind them of it—and *their* only task is to remember it and put it into practice. How convenient! What do we human beings like more than to act in accordance with what we ourselves both know and think? In short, the community that Paul aims to establish has already been realized. So much more important is it to practice it! Note how closely this particular feature fits the understanding of Paul's exhortation (his "paraenesis") that we articulated in chapter 2. It is all about reminding the addressees of something they already know.

This model is already in place in 1 Thessalonians. Once Paul has described the reception he originally received from the Thessalonians (1:2–10), he introduces his account of his own behavior toward them (2:1–12) in the following way (2:1):

> **T5.33** [1]*You yourselves know*, brothers, that our coming to you was not in vain.

And he continues like this (2:9–11):

> **T5.34** [9]*You remember* our labor and toil, brothers. . . . [10]*You are yourselves witnesses*, and God also. . . . [11]*As you know*, . . .

After all this, we at long last get the introduction to the second half of the letter, in which Paul turns to exhorting the Thessalonians on a number of points. Will they then learn something new? Not at all (4:1–2):

> **T5.35** [1]Finally, brothers, we ask and exhort you in the Lord Jesus that, *as you learned from us* how you ought to live and to please God

> (*as, in fact, you are doing*), you should do so *more and more.* [2]For *you know* what instructions we gave you through the Lord Jesus.

He continues (4:9–10),

> **T5.36** [9]Now concerning love of the brothers, you do not need to have anyone write to you, *for you yourselves have been taught* by God to love one another; [10]and indeed you do love all the brothers throughout Macedonia. But we exhort you, beloved, to do so *more and more.*

In short, they already do it; only, they need to do it even more.

At this point, we need to consider the translation "exhort" of the Greek verb that Paul uses: *parakaleín*. Paul employs this term in two contexts. There are texts like **T5.35** and **T5.36** where the translation "exhort" feels natural. But there are other texts like the praise of God at the beginning of 2 Corinthians (**T5.28**) where the traditional translation is "consolation," which I have myself also adopted. However, Paul himself employs the same term (*parakaleín*) in both contexts. A better translation into English would be "encourage," since this covers both contexts. In 1 Thessalonians, Paul "encourages" his addressees to live and act in the manner they already know. He does not in fact *exhort* them in a moralizing way as if they were presented with something new. In 2 Corinthians, God has himself "encouraged" Paul in such a way that his affliction has turned into joy. God does not literally *console* Paul in a sentimental manner as if he were a child.

Paul is often understood as a moralizer. It is true that he wishes his addressees to live "in accordance with the gospel of Christ" (as he says in Phil 1:27). But he is not just moralizing. His exhortations are *encouragements*: reminders about living and acting in the ways they already know, the ways that *follow* from their Christ faith. Paul aims to integrate, not to estrange.

There is no need to give more examples of Paul's encouragements vis-à-vis his addressees. They are innumerable. That is why it makes sense to see Paul's letters in terms of their genre as letters of encouragement (*paráklēsis*, from *parakaleín*). Their purpose is to encourage the addressees to live concretely in the ways that are in accordance with the Christ gospel by reminding them of these ways: they already know them.

What, then, is the relationship in this between what we would call theology and what we would call ethics? Does it all fall under Paul's practice of encouragement, or is this only concerned with ethics? One might take it the latter way, which would make the theology serve only as a *justification* for the ethics. In fact, the theology does serve that way in Paul. But he may also speak of encouragement in connection with themes that are distinctly theological. Chapter 4 of 1 Thessalonians is a good example. He begins with the text in **T5.35** (4:1–2), which is concerned with how the Thessalonians should live concretely—that is, with ethics. This is continued in **T5.36** (4:9–10). In between (4:3–8, **T1.10**), Paul has explained how the Thessalonian brothers should have sex: exclusively with their wives and "in holiness and honor" (4:4)! This is also about ethics. Nevertheless, he concludes the chapter (4:13–17, **T0.1**) on a more theological note by explaining how the Thessalonians should understand the fact that against their expectations, some among them have died *before* Christ has returned. He ends like this (4:18):

> T5.37 18Therefore, encourage one another with these words.

In other words, even an exclusively theological issue like the one about the manner of Christ's return becomes an occasion for Paul to provide mutual encouragement to his addressees. Thus Paul's letters are fundamentally letters of encouragement.

The present point, however, is that in his whole way of writing his letters, Paul is primarily aiming to integrate his addressees both concretely with himself (that is the direct rhetorical function) and also at a much deeper level with the community of love—based in Christ faith—which is the apostle's overall theme.

PAUL AND CHRIST AS EXAMPLES TO BE IMITATED

Encouragement was understood in antiquity as a specific literary genre that included a number of different literary motifs. It was often found precisely in letters. One literary tool in letters of encouragement was the use of human examples or models to be imitated for the purpose of showing the addressees exactly what they were encouraged to do. Paul regularly uses two such examples: himself and Christ. The great model is of course Christ; a somewhat smaller one (but only *slightly* smaller!) is Paul himself. In fact, Paul from time to time almost presents himself *as* Christ, which is not without its point. Not only are Paul and Christ in principle identical (through the pneuma): in both cases, the purpose of presenting them as examples is that by imitating them, the addressees, on their side, should become identical with the two. Paul's whole agenda lies in bringing his addressees into that kind of genuine community between themselves, Paul, and Christ.

Once again, we may begin with 1 Thessalonians. In the introductory thanksgiving section (1:2–10), in which Paul both thanks God and praises the Thessalonians for their manner of receiving him, he introduces the notion of imitation (1:6, see in **T5.7**):

> (T5.7) [6]And you *became imitators* of us and of the Lord when you received the word in great affliction (but also) in joy in the holy pneuma.

Later, Paul will compare the Thessalonians with the Christ believers in Judea (2:14):

> **T5.38** [14]For you, brothers, *became imitators* of the congregations of God in Christ Jesus that are in Judea, for you suffered the same things from your own compatriots as they did from the Jews.

Even though the Thessalonians have imitated different people or groups, in both cases, it is the afflictions of these people that they have imitated.

However, that is not always the case. As we already partly know (see chapter 3), 1 Corinthians chapters 8–10 contain a long and complicated discussion of the issue of whether the Christ-believing Corinthians are allowed to eat meat together with their non-Christ-believing friends if the meat may derive from a sacrifice to pagan idols. Paul concludes the whole discussion like this (1 Cor 10:31–11:1):

> (**T3.7**) [10:31]So, whether you eat or drink, or whatever you do, do everything for the glory of God. [32]Give no offense to Jews or to Greeks or to the church of God, [33]just as I try to please everyone in everything I do, not seeking my own advantage, but that of the many, so that they may be saved. [11:1]*Be imitators of me, as I am of Christ.*

Here we find both the basic idea of imitating Paul, who imitates Christ, and also the underlying idea of exactly what the Corinthians should imitate *in* them. The topic is neither more nor less than Paul's fundamental maxim about thinking of the good of *others*, never of oneself. Christ did this, Paul has done it (in fact, he is now referring back to his account of this in 1 Cor 9:19–23, **T2.13**), and the Corinthians must do it too. That type of behavior ("love") is what constitutes the community that will be established once all imitate Christ.

Another text that speaks of imitation is Philippians 3:17. Paul has described his own change from being a first-class Pharisee who persecuted God's Christ-believing congregation (Phil 3:5–6, see in **T0.9**) to having by now an extremely personal relationship with Christ (Phil 3:7–11):

> **(T0.9)** [7]Yet whatever gains I had, these I have come to regard as loss because of Christ. [8]More than that, I regard everything as loss because of the surpassing value of knowing Christ Jesus my Lord. For his sake I have suffered the loss of all things, and I regard them as rubbish, in order that I may gain Christ [9]and be found in him, not having a righteousness of my own that comes from the law, but one that comes through faith in Christ, the righteousness from God based on faith, [10]in order that I may know Christ and the power of his resurrection and the sharing of his sufferings by becoming like him in his death, [11]if somehow I may attain the resurrection from the dead.

This text, which is one of the Pauline purple passages, is high-strung, compact, and asking the reader to weigh every single word in it. Unfortunately, that cannot be done here. In what follows (3:12–16, **T6.1**), Paul asserts that he does not believe that he himself has reached the final goal. He only pursues it, and he enjoins the Philippians to do the same. Then it comes (3:17),

> **T5.39** [17]Brothers, *join in imitating together with me.*

Once again, Paul invokes the imitation of himself. But since in what precedes (see **T0.9**, just quoted), he has described how he himself attempts to become one with Christ, this is also where he aims to lead the Philippians. They are precisely urged to join *together with* him in imitating—Christ. Here, too, we see that what is ultimately at stake is the community of love among *all* involved: the addressees, Paul himself, *and* Christ.

CREATING SOCIAL REALITY THROUGH WORDS

Apart from Romans, all Paul's letters were written to people he knew from the time when he had persuaded them to form local congregations of Christ believers. The basic purpose of the letters is to maintain these Christ believers in the state they were in when Paul left them. The letters presuppose a distinct social reality, which they aim to strengthen. That is why they are letters of encouragement.

But we also know that the letters were intended to intervene in relation to specific problems that had arisen after Paul had left the congregations, problems that precisely threatened to undermine the social reality that had previously been established. The letters therefore also want to guide the congregations to avoid this breakdown by solving the problems. However, although the solutions offered by Paul may appear very much ad hoc, they remain anchored in the overall understanding that was present to begin with. It is this basic understanding to which Paul appeals when he attempts to solve the problems that had arisen after his departure.

In spite of this, Paul does more in his letters than merely remind his addressees of what they already know or show them how new answers and solutions may be derived from that. He writes in a manner that literally aims to *recreate* the social reality that was there at his departure—as if it had already to some extent broken down. Paul has several ways of doing this. One is to make clear to his addressees that they are part of a movement that is much larger than themselves. This happens, for instance, when he mentions his co-workers in his letter greetings or when he in general speaks of "God's congregation" as something much larger than the individual congregation. If the whole thing is not just about you but about something much bigger, then you will of course stand together with all the others! A second approach is to bring himself into the game by describing how he reaches out for his addressees. When Paul on his side does this, surely they will respond in the same way! A third approach is to describe in his own case the radical and all-encompassing character of the confession to Christ. If the addressees will actually *experience* this (through Paul's account of it), then they, too, will join in (again)!

What is common to all these approaches is that they are all directed toward a single end, which is the realization of a complete community between the addressees, Paul, and Christ. It is this (imagined) social reality that all Paul's literary artifice in the letters is intended to strengthen and even to recreate.

Note then—this is what I have been aiming to show—the degree to which Paul's various ways of reaching this goal in themselves *reflect* the goal. If the goal is a community of love—as realized and imagined—between all involved, then Paul must speak to his addressees in a manner that both reflects and presupposes such a community. And so he does. That is the case, for instance, when he includes others than himself in his address, when he basically only encourages his addressees, and when he only employs himself and Christ as examples. It is also the case when he constantly attempts to *argue* his cause—as, for instance, in his discussion of women's head covering during service (1 Cor 11:2–16, **T4.5–9**), as we saw in the preceding chapter. In these ways, he leaves it *up to the addressees* to respond in the intended manner. Thus Paul's rhetoric itself *expresses* his maxim. He himself follows it in his rhetorical practice.

In the next chapter, we will see that this is far from everything that should be said about Paul's rhetorical practice of persuasion. Up to now, we have only been looking at his ways of addressing people he takes to be already on the inside. He speaks very differently to those people he takes to be on the outside—or to those he thinks *risk* getting there.

* * *

Suppose we have diagnosed correctly in this chapter the character of Paul's writerly practice. In that case, we must speak of a very high degree of rhetorical awareness in Paul concerning not just the means to adopt in order to reach his goals but also something deeper. What we have seen is, first, that Paul understood how certain forms of rhetorical practice hang together and reflect the very *content* that his rhetoric was intended to bring about and, second, that he himself *practiced* this insight. If the content consisted in a genuine community, then the rhetoric must reflect that. Then it could not just make use of propaganda or seduction. Nor could it make use of psychic violence, for instance, by building on the special authority of the apostle and attempting to force the addressees into submission. Instead, it must *appeal*—and appeal to the addressees' *own* understanding. That is an aspect of Paul's use of rhetoric that I myself find quite moving. When are we ourselves able to practice what we preach, particularly when we feel that everything is at stake?

As already noted, this is far from everything that should be said about Paul's rhetoric. But it *is* a central mark of his writerly practice. What is more, it is something that we ourselves may employ without further ado. What Paul practices toward those he considers to be on the inside is a mixture of attentiveness to the views of others, of genuine argumentation, and of tolerance toward others. And behind it lies this idea: we *have* to come together in the kind of community that is at stake; let us then *together* find out what it consists in and how we may get there.

Where did he get these ideas and this practice? The answer must without doubt be this: directly from the experience of the community of love that Christ-dead-and-resurrected, according to Paul, meant.

Thus Paul was not just a faith fanatic (and a philosopher). He was also a practitioner of faith.

6

THE PERSUASION

EXCLUSION

IN THE PRECEDING chapter, we considered a number of examples of Paul's attempt to integrate his addressees in the Christ community for which he was arguing, including his use of himself for the same purpose. This is all a matter of Paul's rhetoric: his use of language in the letters in order to achieve certain goals. It is important to see that this also holds for his account of himself. Paul is constantly engaged in constructing an image of himself—what we may call his *persona*. And that, too, serves certain purposes. We can only guess how this image relates to Paul's own real person behind it all. When, in what follows, I speak of Paul's person, what I have in mind is in principle the *persona* that he constructs through his writing.

In spite of this, it is difficult to get rid of the sense that there is a reasonably direct connection between Paul's *persona* as expressed in the letters and the apostle himself. So it is perhaps not wholly wrong if the reader of Paul gets the feeling that one is here in fairly direct contact with an exceedingly complex human being of flesh and blood—across two thousand years.

I had written the previous sentence when I came across a statement made in August 2019 by the French novelist Michel Houellebecq: "What is unusual about Paul is that one gets the feeling of getting very close to him. When I read Paul, I have the sense that he is standing right there next to me so that I can almost hear him breathe." I would not perhaps myself put it quite so extravagantly, but there is something to it. This is one reason we will go slightly more into detail in this chapter about two letters in which Paul reveals himself particularly clearly: Galatians and 2 Corinthians.

In any case, the *persona* that Paul manages to bring across in these two letters is his strongest bid at making us understand the overall Christ identity that he aims to generate in his congregations. For this reason, too, the two letters call for our full attention.

THE MOVEMENT TOWARD EXCLUSION

Our theme in this chapter is Paul's rhetorical practice when he is moving in the opposite direction of integration: exclusion. This occurs most clearly when he relates to opponents whom he does not see as members of the given congregation but instead as having come to it from the outside. Here he is not working for integration. On the contrary, we here encounter a Paul who is quite radical in his rejection. One must remember, however, that he never addresses such opponents directly. He is always in principle writing *about* them, addressing himself instead directly *to* his congregationalists. They are the people whom he wishes to influence.

His way of addressing *these* people is in fact the more interesting one. In principle, as we saw in the preceding chapter, Paul is integrative toward his addressees. Now, however, we will see that he may also be *potentially* exclusive in his way of addressing them. That happens when he fears that under the influence of the external opponents, they are on their way out.

We thus have three different groups with three different positions within Paul's rhetorical practice. At the center of what we may call the Christ circle (those on the inside) are Christ believers on whom Paul feels he can count. To them he speaks in only integrative ways. Further away from the center but still within the circle are those considered by Paul to be potentially on the way out.

We may call them the undecided. To them he speaks in ways that are partly integrative—not least by reminding them of where they previously were—and also partly exclusive, or at least with a *threat* of exclusion if they do not conform. Finally, there are the direct opponents, who, according to Paul, are outside the Christ circle. These he speaks not *to* but *about*. And here his tone is strongly exclusive. However, since he is not addressing them directly, it is clear that his harsh tone with regard to the direct opponents is in fact aimed at the undecided. *They* must understand the risk they are running.

Paul does not himself speak of a "Christ circle." According to him, one either is or is not "in Christ." However, one text in particular points relatively clearly in the direction of the idea of a Christ circle, within which there is *some* room for differences. The text is Philippians 3:12–16, which follows directly on Paul's account of his own change from living (alone) under the law of Moses to living "in" Christ (3:2–11, **T0.9**). Here is 3:12–16:

> **T6.1** [12]Not that I have already obtained this or have already reached the goal [the resurrection or Christ]; but I press on if only I can grasp it just as I have myself been grasped by Christ Jesus. [13]Beloved, I do not consider that I have made it my own; but this one thing I do: forgetting what lies behind and straining forward to what lies ahead, [14]I press on toward the goal for the prize of the heavenly call of God in Christ Jesus. [15]Let those of us then who are mature be of the same mind; and if you think differently about anything, this too God will reveal to you. [16]Only let us walk in the trail we have already adopted.

All those to whom Paul is here talking are "mature" (in fact, "perfect"; Greek *teleioi*). Still, none of them—neither, in fact, Paul himself—has *completely* reached the goal, as it were at the center of the "Christ circle" that we may imagine. They therefore *may* have (slightly) different views. What matters is that they follow along the same path as far as they have individually gone—and in the same direction (namely, toward the center). It is different, of course, with those who are *not* walking along that path. They belong *outside* the circle. In **T6.1**, Paul does not take into account the undecided. We may ourselves place them where they belong: inside the circle—*but* with a risk of falling out of it.

In the following discussion, we will examine together how Paul relates to both the undecided and the opponents. As we saw, when Paul writes *about* the latter, he has the former in view.

THE UNDECIDED AND THE OPPONENTS IN GALATIANS

In Galatians, the situation, as we know, is that some Jewish preachers of Christ have turned up among the non-Jewish Galatians after Paul's departure with the message that the Galatian men should let themselves be circumcised in order to become real Jews. The newcomers had apparently had some success. The Galatians were now ready to follow their advice. In his letter, Paul speaks to his addressees as if they were all undecided. What procedures does he adopt in addressing them?

In chapter 1, his basic strategy consists in separating himself from the Galatians. We have previously seen (Gal 1:1–5, **T5.5**) that he emphasizes his status as "an apostle—sent neither by human commission nor from human authorities, but through Jesus Christ and God the Father." We have also seen that he replaces the normal thanksgiving with a section expressing his astonishment that the Galatians have so quickly gone over to a different gospel—which does not exist (Gal 1:6–7, see in **T3.1**). Here Paul also refers directly to his opponents as "some who are confusing you." He continues with a characteristic lack of modesty (1:8–9):

> (**T3.1**) [8]But even if *we or an angel from heaven* should proclaim to you a gospel contrary to what we proclaimed to you, let that one

> be accursed! [9]As we have said before, so now I repeat, if anyone proclaims to you a gospel contrary to what you received, let that one be accursed!

Here there is no openness toward the others. Paul (twice!) *hurls* a curse against his opponents—or against the undecided among the Galatians were they to join the others: away with them!

In the rest of chapter 1 (1:10–24), Paul gives an account of his own call that continues his emphasis in the letter greeting that he has been sent directly by God. We may conclude that in this whole text, the apostle is speaking authoritatively to the highest degree. He directly *invokes* God. Nobody may preach a gospel different from the one that Paul has himself received from God.

In chapter 2, Paul continues his account of his own life from the moment he was called until his arrival among the Galatians. Everything here is carefully arranged to show that Paul's own understanding of the gospel to the non-Jewish Galatians is the correct one. They must not submit to the law of Moses by letting themselves be circumcised. Christ faith suffices.

In chapter 3, he at long last gets to the heart of the matter by giving an account of *why* the Galatians must not submit to the law and *how* they should live instead. Into this passage, which constitutes the remainder of the letter, Paul weaves four specific texts in which he addresses the Galatians directly and speaks about their potential defection. These texts are particularly revealing for understanding the apostle's rhetorical strategy.

As so often, he begins with an appeal to the Galatians' own experience of their original conversion (3:1–5):

> **T6.2** [1]You foolish Galatians! Who has bewitched you? It was before your eyes that Jesus Christ was publicly exhibited as crucified! [2]The only thing I want to learn from you is this: Did you receive the pneuma by doing the works of the law or by believing what

> you heard? [3]Are you so foolish? Having started with the pneuma, are you now ending with the flesh? [4]Did you experience so much for nothing?—if it really was for nothing. [5]Well then, does God supply you with the pneuma and work miracles among you by your doing the works of the law, or by your believing what you heard?

In what ways was Christ publicly exhibited as crucified to the eyes of the Galatians? As we will see in a moment (**T6.3** below), the answer is this: when they saw Paul himself, who was apparently seriously ill. Thus Paul goes back to his first visit with them and brings in himself as a kind of substitute for Christ. In addition, he directly appeals to God, who has given them the pneuma and miracle-working powers. The strategy is this: (1) behind Paul, there is God, Christ, and the pneuma, and (2) they themselves experienced it all when they were called.

After a long theological discussion (3:6–4:11), Paul again addresses the Galatians directly in a longer text that tells us a lot about his rhetorical strategy. At the same time, it is one of the texts in which Paul is most actively at work constructing his own rhetorical *persona* (4:12–20):

> **T6.3** [12]Friends, I beg you, become as I am, for I also have become as you are. You have done me no wrong. [13]You know that it was in a state of a physical infirmity that I first announced the gospel to you; [14]though my condition put you to the test, you did not scorn or despise me, but *welcomed me as an angel of God, as Christ Jesus.* [15]What has become of the goodwill you felt? For I testify that, had it been possible, you would have torn out your eyes and given them to me. [16]Have I now become your enemy by telling you the truth? [17]*They* make much of you, but for no good purpose; they want to exclude you, so that you may make much of them. [18]It is good to be

> made much of for a good purpose at all times, and not only when I am present with you, [19]my little children, for whom I am again in the pain of childbirth until Christ is formed in you. [20]I wish I were present with you now and could change my tone, for I am perplexed about you.

This text contains a number of strategic motifs. There is the idea of an identity between the apostle and the addressees (4:12). There is a reminder of an illness that might have tempted the Galatians to despise Paul at the time of their original conversion but that had the opposite effect (4:13–14). There is the idea that at the time, the Galatians saw Paul as either an angel from God or Jesus Christ himself (4:14). There is the suggestion that the Galatians were prepared to give Paul the most precious thing they had (their eyes) in gratitude for his preaching. There is the violent account of what the Galatians *might* have done but precisely did not (4:14; 4:15). There is the claim that the opponents want to separate Paul from the Galatians (4:17). There is the idea that Paul has to give birth to the Galatians once more so that Christ may once again be formed in them (4:19). Finally, there is the implicit appeal deriving from the fact that Paul (their original mother!) is at his wit's end about them (4:20).

What runs through all this is a strong appeal, almost a cry. They *were* so excellent; Paul on his side continues to be totally open toward them: Why, then, has he become their enemy? Why do they not respond as they did then? In short, "I am perplexed about you." Note also that Paul himself indicates that he is speaking in a different tone from the usual one: "I wish I . . . could change my tone" (4:20). The difference is due to the fact that he cannot now trust that they are still on the inside. That is why he appeals to them as intensely as he can, using a strongly pathetic language: come, come, come!

Is Paul, then, also potentially exclusive? On the contrary! He attempts to employ language that is as integrative as it can be. And the *persona* that he builds up is a complex one of an apostle who in his Christlike character is admittedly, on the negative side, pestered by his opponents—but is also on the strongly positive side even in pains of labor from having to give birth once more to Christ in his immediate addressees. What holds Paul's *persona* together in this text is that it is so intensely focused on the addressees. It is for their sake that Paul sees and depicts himself the way he does. His openness toward them is total (4:12, see in **T6.3**):

> (**T6.3**) [12]Friends, I beg you, become as I am, for I also have become as you are.

One may like this or not, but it is surely very powerful rhetorically. Who does not want to be courted in this way?

The third text in which Paul addresses the Galatians directly has a different character. It comes just after Paul has summarized his theological message to the effect that through Christ faith, his non-Jewish addressees are free from the law of Moses (5:1–6). He continues like this (5:7–12):

> **T6.4** [7]You were running well; who prevented you from obeying the truth? [8]Such persuasion does not come from the one who calls you. [9]A little yeast leavens the whole batch of dough. [10]I am confident about you in the Lord that you will not think otherwise. But whoever it is that is confusing you will pay the penalty. [11]But brothers, why am I still being persecuted if I am still preaching circumcision? In that case, the offense of the cross has been removed. [12]I wish those who unsettle you would themselves cut the whole thing off!

It is strong tobacco when the apostle of Christ concludes this text by expressing his pious wish that his opponents, who are arguing for circumcision, may end up castrating themselves! Paul is evidently under strong pressure. This is reflected in a mixture in the immediately preceding verses of perplexity with regard to the Galatians and rejection of the opponents. In both cases, he employs an abrupt style consisting of almost telegraphically short sentences. The perplexity comes out clearly in 5:7–9. Paul simply cannot understand why his addressees have let themselves be convinced by the opponents. Gradually, he therefore turns his gaze toward the latter. Like a small leaven, they risk corrupting the whole dough (5:9)—that is, all the Galatians. This leads him to a direct rejection of the opponents (5:10b). However, in spite of his declaration to the contrary (5:10a), he cannot be certain that the Galatians will end up having the right view. This uncertainty underlies 5:11: Has anybody (presumably the opponents) told them and do they themselves believe that Paul continues to preach circumcision? Never! For why should he then himself be persecuted—namely, *by* the opponents? In addition, that would mean that the "offence of the cross" would have been abolished. In short, if they think so, they are totally off the track. And then back to rejecting the opponents: I wish that they would cut the whole thing off (5:12)!

We should conclude that whereas **T6.3** was strongly integrative in relation to the Galatians in spite of Paul's perplexity about them, **T6.4** begins from the same perplexity but gradually moves toward a stance of a complete rejection and exclusion in relation to the opponents. Still, the text continues to be addressed *to* the Galatians. Thus by inveighing against his opponents, Paul attempts to put the strongest possible pressure on the Galatians. They must choose between either side.

Again, whether one likes it or not, this is all rhetorically highly effective. But it also shows an apostle who is himself under pressure. The *persona* that Paul constructs here is that of an apostle who is baffled by his addressees' departure from the truth ("You were running well") but nevertheless takes up a stance of direct confrontation with those who are disturbing them (they "will pay the penalty"). His reaction to the uncertain situation in Galatia leaves no room for wavering: *he* knows, the Galatians have been seduced, the opponents will be punished.

The fourth and last text in which Paul addresses the Galatians directly (6:8–11) summarizes everything that precedes it by going back to Paul's self-presentation in chapter 1. This is where he writes with "large letters" (6:11):

> **(T5.10)** [11]See what large letters I make when I am writing in my own hand!

He continues by caricaturing his opponents (6:12–13) and placing himself in radical opposition to them (6:14–15):

> **(T0.6)** [12]It is those who want to make a good showing in the flesh that try to compel you to be circumcised—only that they may not be persecuted for the cross of Christ. [13]Even the circumcised [or those who preach circumcision] do not themselves obey the law, but they want you to be circumcised so that they may boast about your flesh. [14]I, by contrast, may I never boast of anything except the cross of our Lord Jesus Christ, by which the world has been crucified to me, and I to the world. [15]For neither circumcision nor uncircumcision is anything; but a new creation is everything!

First, on the caricaturing: the opponents only wish to make a good appearance (vis-à-vis their Jewish compatriots), they only wish to avoid being persecuted (by the same people) for Christ's cross, they only want to boast (toward the same people) of your flesh. Then the radical opposition: I on my side. . . . Next Paul produces one of his radical interpretive inversions of "the cross of Christ," which we already studied in chapter 1. This is one of the most striking examples of Paul's constructing a *persona* for himself.

On the one side stands the whole world, including the opponents and their notions of value. On the other side stands Christ's cross—and Paul himself, who has been *crucified* to the world! For him, this cross is the *only* thing that matters. Indeed, it signifies a completely new creation of the human being. *Everything* else—including being circumcised (a Jew) or uncircumcised (a non-Jew)—is wholly indifferent.

What we see here is the extent to which Paul anchors his own identity in a single place (with God, focusing on Christ's death on the cross)—and correspondingly rejects all other notions of value and identity. It is a complete either-or. Moreover, the *persona* that Paul constructs is that of somebody standing *alone* with his back to the wall. Of course, Paul is still addressing the Galatians, hoping that they may come over to his side, which is the only correct one. But so far, there is only one person there: Paul.

The double strategy of Paul insisting on himself alone but nevertheless also extending a hand to the Galatians is repeated in the two final verses of the letter (6:17–18):

> (**T0.7**) 17From now on, let no one make trouble for me; for I carry the marks of Jesus branded on my body. 18May the grace of our Lord Jesus Christ be with your spirit, brothers. Amen.

Galatians 6:18 is the traditional letter closure, whose function is clearly integrative. But 6:17 is the apex of Paul's (potentially) exclusive practice: there he stands, *completely* alone—but evidently also with Christ and God behind him. He, Paul, is carrying the marks of Jesus branded on his own body! What he is actually referring to here is quite unclear. Perhaps the reference is to the illness he mentioned in **T6.3**. But the image itself is a stark one—and (potentially) completely exclusive.

In the four passages of Galatians that we have considered, Paul builds up a specific *persona* that—if we take it literally—is a tragic one. On the one hand, he is completely certain about himself, his cause, and the sense that he has God and Christ directly behind him. On the other hand, he is persecuted by opponents, whom he curses and over whom he wishes everything bad. Also, he is in fact totally uncertain about his addressees. What he ends up insisting on is his own Christ identity, which also *should* be that of his addressees: that he is crucified to the world and that nobody must trouble him, since he carries Jesus's stigmata. Truly, a tragic *persona*!

THE UNDECIDED IN 1 CORINTHIANS

In 1 Corinthians, Paul's tone toward his addressees is relatively confident. For instance, the thanksgiving section (1:4–9) is exclusively positive. There is no end to all the things for which one must thank God in their regard. In spite of this, there is a need for some encouragement (1:10–13):

> **T6.5** [10]Now I appeal to you, brothers, by the name of our Lord Jesus Christ, that all of you be in agreement and that there be no divisions among you, but that you be united in the same mind and the same understanding. [11]For it has been reported to me by Chloe's people that there are quarrels among you, my brothers. [12]What I mean is that each of you says, "I belong to Paul," or "I belong to Apollos," or "I belong to Cephas [i.e., Peter]," or "I belong to Christ." [13]Has Christ been divided? Was Paul crucified for you? Or were you baptized in the name of Paul?

The Corinthian congregation is obviously divided and, as becomes clear later, not just on the question to whose party they belong.

In the rest of the letter, Paul attempts to settle these differences by drawing on a range of theological motifs. The basis is laid in chapters 1–4. Once more, it consists in the crucifixion of Jesus, which is a foolishness to the Greeks and a scandal to the Jews

(1:23). By contrast, to those who are called and have received God's pneuma—whether Jews or non-Jews—it is an expression of the deepest wisdom and of God's power (1:24). Paul develops all this in a manner he has not been able to do previously (3:1–4):

> **T6.6** [1]And so, brothers, I could not speak to you as pneumatic people, but rather as people of the flesh, as infants in Christ. [2]I fed you with milk, not solid food, for you were not ready for solid food. Even now you are still not ready, [3]for you are still of the flesh. For as long as there is jealousy and quarreling among you, are you not of the flesh, and behaving according to human inclinations? [4]For when one says, "I belong to Paul," and another, "I belong to Apollos," are you not merely human?

Thus in 1 Corinthians, too, Paul is confronted with other preachers, here one Apollos, of whom we do not know much. However, he at least has a name, and he is not presented as a direct opponent of Paul in the way we have met in Galatians—and will meet again in 2 Corinthians. Apollos plays a certain role in chapters 3–4 of 1 Corinthians—though primarily as a means for Paul to address the Corinthians directly and criticize their divisions. Paul first introduces himself as an example of the correct type of "servants of Christ and stewards of God's mysteries" (4:1). Such people must first of all be trustworthy (4:2). Then he continues (4:3–5),

> **T6.7** [3]But with me it is a very small thing that I should be judged by you or by any human court. I do not even judge myself. [4]I am not aware of anything against myself, but I am not thereby acquitted. It is the Lord who judges me. [5]Therefore, do not pronounce judgement before the time, before the Lord comes, who will bring to light the things now hidden in darkness and will disclose the purposes of the heart. Then each one will receive commendation from God.

The point is obvious: the Corinthians must not engage in judging the various preachers like Paul himself or Apollos. For it is the Lord (Christ) and God himself who will judge them on the day of judgment. And Paul feels sure that he will himself pass that test.

Again, Paul constructs a *persona* of an apostle with a strong self-consciousness vis-à-vis his addressees, a self-consciousness that may at least potentially separate them from one another. In fact, he here speaks in a manner that is highly authoritative and potentially gives them the cold shoulder. Once he has spelled out his point, he confronts the Corinthians even more directly, this time through the use of irony and one of those interpretive inversions in which he specializes. This is Paul building up his *persona* to great effect (4:6–13):

> **T6.8** [6]I have applied all this to Apollos and myself for your benefit, brothers, so that you may learn through us the meaning of the saying, "Nothing beyond what is written," so that none of you will be puffed up in favor of one against another. [7]For who sees anything special in you? What do you have that you did not receive? And if you received it, why do you boast as if it were not a gift? [8]Already you are full up! Already you have become rich! Quite apart from us you have become kings! Indeed, I wish that you had become kings, so that we might be kings with you! [9]For I think that God has exhibited us apostles as last of all, as though sentenced to death, because we have become a spectacle to the world, to angels and to mortals. [10]*We* are fools for the sake of Christ, but *you* are wise in Christ. *We* are weak, but *you* are strong. *You* are held in honor, but *we* in disrepute. [11]To the present hour we are hungry and thirsty, we are poorly clothed and beaten and homeless, [12]and we grow weary from the work of our own hands. When reviled, we bless; when persecuted, we endure; [13]when slandered, we speak kindly. We have become like the rubbish of the world, the dregs of all things, to this very day.

What is Paul doing here? He censures the Corinthians for believing that each of them is in possession of the truth so that they are able to criticize others with whom they disagree. They think that they are already "full up," "rich," and "kings"—in other words, that with the knowledge they have, they also have a high status in an ordinary social context. But, says Paul, if they do have something, it is something they have *received* (from God). That requires some humility. And were they to take "us apostles" as an example, they would see something entirely different: the lowest conceivable status—which Paul is then happy to spell out in the strongest possible terms. The apostles are like people condemned to death in an arena where the whole world from the highest to the lowest is sitting applauding. They are rubbish; they are dregs. What should the Corinthians learn from this? Precisely, mutual humility among one another so that they will no longer engage in strife but instead be "in agreement and that there be no divisions among you, but that you be united in the same mind and the same understanding" (1:10, see in **T6.5**).

That is the conclusion one should draw from Christ's death on the cross. And that is what Paul focuses on in the present context, in which the Corinthians have shown themselves to be like ordinary human beings of flesh and blood. But is that all? Is Paul just exhorting them to be despised scum in an ordinary social context, just as their apostles are (and behind them, of course, the crucified Christ)? Not at all! He ironically declares that they are *already* full up (etc.). And he twice declares that "we [the apostles]" suffer innumerable afflictions "to the present hour" and "to this very day." The point is that the present low status of both the apostles and the Corinthians will in the future be transformed into one of the highest status when the crucifixion of Christ reaches its goal in the resurrection toward which it is pointing: the resurrection of *all*, which has been anticipated in Christ's own resurrection. However, we are not yet there. What is required *now* in present practice is the mutual humility that matches the crucifixion of Christ.

So far, we may conclude that Paul directly censures the Corinthians for behaving like ordinary human beings of flesh and blood and that he attempts, by his own example and *persona*, to draw the proper lessons from the crucifixion of Christ. We may also note that Paul addresses them highly ironically. They *think* they are full up and so on, but of course they are not. Is Paul, then, here speaking to them in a manner that is integrative or (potentially) exclusive? At least partly the first. After all, the use of irony presupposes that they are able to understand it and to adjust their course accordingly.

We should also take note of Paul's description of himself in the latter half of **T6.8**, in particular 4:11–13, since it is so strongly characteristic of him. He is building up an image of his own *persona* as an apostle: like one who is condemned to death in the arena, despised, maltreated, and so on. Note then the striking change in the middle of 4:12. *However*, when reviled, we bless and so on. The point is that all the afflictions that the apostles (and in principle all Christ believers) experience are in the end completely irrelevant in comparison with something that is much bigger and that they already possess: that *they* will at some point be full up, rich, and kings! That is what empowers them to react to ordinary human afflictions—to which they are exposed in the usual system of values—in a manner that is wholly unusual within that system. They literally turn the other cheek to those afflictions, as Jesus had also stated they should. Even more, they *bless* their tormentors! Once more, the central element in Paul's *persona* is that he is totally conformed with the crucified Jesus Christ.

The conclusion to chapter 4 shows that Paul is fully aware of the question of which tone of voice he should adopt. He continues like this (4:14–21):

> **T6.9** [14]I am not writing this to make you ashamed, but to admonish you as my beloved children. [15]For though you might have ten thousand guardians in Christ, you do not have many fathers.

> Indeed, in Christ Jesus *I* became your father through the gospel.
> [16]I encourage you, then, be imitators of me. [17]For this reason I sent
> you Timothy, who is my beloved and faithful child in the Lord, to
> remind you of my ways in Christ Jesus, as I teach them everywhere
> in every church. [18]But some of you, thinking that I am not coming
> to you, have become arrogant. [19]But I will come to you soon, if the
> Lord wills, and I will find out not the talk of these arrogant people
> but their power. [20]For the kingdom of God depends not on talk but
> on power. [21]What would you prefer? Am I to come to you with a
> stick, or with love in a pneuma of gentleness?

In this passage, Paul at first speaks in an integrative manner to all the Corinthians. They all have Paul as their father in Christ, since he was the one who converted them. Recalling Galatians 4:19 (in **T6.3**), we may note in passing that in Paul's *persona*, he could be both a father and a mother to his addressees. It is all about birthing them in one form or another. As the Corinthians' father, he has no other wish than to exhort and encourage them to imitate him. That is also the reason he has sent Timothy to them. Paul loves Timothy, and his task is to remind the Corinthians of Paul's own ways in Christ. This is all integrative, an expression of the pneuma of love and mildness that he mentions at the end.

But then there are also *some* Corinthians who puff themselves up. They are the people who were mentioned in 4:6 (see in **T6.8**), people who create divisions "in favor of one against another." How, Paul asks, should he treat them? Integratively? Or with the stick? It is obvious that this question itself has an integrative function. The idea is that the mutinous Corinthians will themselves most probably understand and so prefer that the issue be solved in mildness. Should that not happen, however, the idea is also that were Paul in fact to employ the stick, the Corinthians would most likely end up conforming and thus continue to be members of the congregation. In all this, it is clear that Paul thinks that the kind of guidance he might be required to give should basically have the character of encouragement in the pneuma of love and mildness. That would directly reflect the community of love that is the core of his overall message. But the "father's" love also *might* call for the stick. Is that what they want?

Thus understood, the whole of Paul's rhetorical strategy in 1 Corinthians 1–4 properly belongs in chapter 5 of this book. We have discussed it here, since we will make use of what we now know about Paul's rhetorical strategy in his first letter to the Corinthians in connection with the next letter he sent to them. Somebody who knows 2 Corinthians, in which Paul is under heavy pressure, may well expect that his strategy in that letter will differ markedly from the one in the earlier letter. In fact, we will see otherwise.

THE UNDECIDED AND THE OPPONENTS IN 2 CORINTHIANS

We already know that the whole first half (chapters 1–7) of 2 Corinthians is made up of one long integrative piece. Paul was (*strongly!*) worried about the Corinthians, and on his way from Asia (Turkey) to Europe (Macedonia), he went through in his thought how sincere and blameless he had been in his apostleship toward them. So much the greater was the consolation and joy he experienced when Titus brought good news from Corinth. As he concludes (7:16),

> (T5.32) 16*I rejoice*, in that I may have complete confidence in you.

However, in the rest of the letter—not least the last four chapters (10–13)—the tone is quite different, so different that many scholars have felt (wrongly, as I believe) that what we have in the canonical letter is at least two different letters. In this part of the letter, Paul describes the Corinthians as almost undecided and for the same reason speaks much more directly about certain people whom he sees as his opponents. We should first ask how he treats these two parties and then ask how the letter as a whole may—in spite of the difference in tone in its two halves—be seen to hang closely together. We will spend a little more time on this, since it is here, where Paul is under severe pressure, that we get closest to him. At the same time, we will once more see that he builds up as his own *persona* a Christ identity that should actually belong to the Corinthians too.

The introduction (10:1–11, see below) to the four chapters immediately shows the difficult situation in which Paul finds himself. The opponents have clearly made an impression on the Corinthians, not so much in terms of specific points of (theological) content as in a direct attack on Paul. In this, the situation differs quite a bit from the one in Galatians. In Corinth, the conflict is over the personal character of the various preachers. For instance, the Corinthian opponents, as we saw in the introduction, have declared that Paul's "letters are weighty and strong, but his bodily presence is weak, and his speech contemptible" (10:10, see **T0.5**). In being confronted with this, Paul's immediate strategy is to distinguish between, on the one side, the Corinthians as a group and, on the other side, the opponents and those among the Corinthians on whom they have made an impression. The former he wishes to build up; the latter he will tear down—unless they are persuaded. And he will do so not just in his letters but also in person when he visits them. Here is the text (10:1–11):

> **T6.10** [1]I myself, Paul, appeal to you by the meekness and gentleness of Christ—I who am humble when face to face with you, but bold toward you when I am away! [2]I ask that when I am present I need not show boldness *with the daring with which I intend* to oppose those who think we are acting according to the flesh. [3]Indeed, we live in the flesh, but we do not wage war according to the flesh; [4]for the weapons of our warfare are not according to the flesh, but they have divine power to destroy strongholds. We destroy arguments [5]and every

proud obstacle raised up against the knowledge of God, and we take every thought captive to obey Christ. [6]We are ready to punish every disobedience—once *your* obedience is complete. [7]Look at what is before your eyes. If somebody is confident that he belongs to Christ, let him remind himself of this, that just as he belongs to Christ, so also do we. [8]Now, even if I boast a little too much of our authority, which the Lord gave for building you up and not for tearing you down, I will not be put to shame. [9]I do not want to seem as though I am (only) trying to frighten you with my *letters*. [10]For somebody says, "His letters are weighty and strong, but his bodily presence is weak, and his speech contemptible." [11]Let such a person understand that what we say by letter when absent, we will also do when present.

After this forceful beginning, the apostle continues by ironically declaring that he would never dare to compare himself with his direct, external opponents, who happily engage in comparing themselves with others. For in being the first one to reach and convert the Corinthians, Paul has only done what God had stipulated. And it is the result that counts. He concludes (10:18),

T6.11 [18]It is not those who commend themselves that are approved, but those whom the Lord commends.

Then follows a longer text (11:1–12:10) in which Paul nevertheless does engage in a close comparison with his external opponents concerning who has most to boast of. He himself characterizes this whole operation as "foolishness" (11:1). For the same reason, he introduces his comparison by asking the Corinthians in an ironically phrased prayer to put up with his self-praise—after all, they put up with so much (11:1–4):

T6.12 [1]I wish you would bear with me in a little foolishness. Surely, you do bear with me! [2]For I feel a divine jealousy for you,

> since I promised you in marriage to one husband, to present you as a chaste virgin to Christ. [3]But I am afraid that as the serpent deceived Eve by its cunning, your thoughts will be led astray from a sincere and pure devotion to Christ. [4]For if someone *comes* [from the outside] *and* proclaims another Jesus than the one we proclaimed, or if you receive a different pneuma from the one you received, or a different gospel from the one you accepted, you bear with it readily enough.

In other words, if they are able to put up with the ghastly message of other people, then they will no doubt also be prepared to put up with a little foolishness on Paul's part. For he has preached Christ to them in sincerity and purity. Here Paul produces a piece of gentle irony that also insists on the radical difference between his own preaching, which is sincere and pure, and that of his opponents, which is anything but that.

When he then finally turns to the comparison he has so laboriously introduced, Paul does not hold back. They are "super-apostles" (11:5); even more (11:13–15),

> **T6.13** [13]such boasters are false apostles, deceitful workers, disguising themselves as apostles of Christ. [14]And no wonder! Even Satan disguises himself as an angel of light [Lucifer]. [15]So it is not strange if his ministers also disguise themselves as ministers of righteousness. Their end will match their deeds.

But of course Paul does not *want* to compare himself with them! So he feels that he must apologize one more time, which he does with the same gentle irony as in **T6.12** (11:16–21):

> **T6.14** [16]I repeat, let no one think that I am a fool; but if you do, then accept me as a fool, so that I too may boast a little. [17]What I am saying in regard to this boastful confidence, I am saying

> not with the Lord's authority, but as a fool; [18]since many boast according to the flesh, I will also boast. [19]For you gladly bear with fools, being wise yourselves! [20]For you bear with it when someone makes slaves of you, or preys upon you, or takes advantage of you, or puts on airs, or gives you a slap in the face. [21]To my shame, I must say, we were too weak for that!

The core of the self-praise in which Paul engages from this point is partly that he has just as many things to boast of as his rivals, partly that *he* boasts of the *right* things—namely, all the *afflictions* that he has suffered in preaching the gospel. As he says (11:30),

> **T6.15** [30]If I must boast, I will boast of the things that show my weakness.

Even when it comes to "visions and revelations of the Lord" (12:1), what he ends up mentioning is a physical illness he has received from Christ (we unfortunately do not know what he is referring to) "to keep me from being too elated" (12:7) by the same visions and revelations. And he concludes as follows (12:9–10):

> **T6.16** [9]So, I will boast all the more gladly of my weaknesses, so that the power of Christ [i.e., the pneuma] may dwell in me. [10]Therefore, I am content with weaknesses, insults, hardships, persecutions, and calamities for the sake of Christ; for whenever I am weak, then I am strong.

We know the model from 1 Corinthians (4:10–13, see in **T6.8**). Weakness, according to the value system of the world, is in reality strength and power in Christ. And that is what the Christ identity consists in. Thus Paul may conclude the whole of his self-description as follows (12:11):

> **T6.17** [11]I have been a fool! You forced me to it. Indeed you should have been the ones commending me, for I am not at all inferior to these super-apostles, even though I am nothing.

In this text, Paul summarizes the two sides of the preceding, long text. First, he has been forced to boast of all his merits, since the Corinthians have not been prepared to recommend him but have instead been running after those who have recommended themselves. Second, he is in no way left behind by his opponents *precisely* when he is himself nothing whatsoever. Once again, it is the idea of Christ's crucifixion (the weakest imaginable event) that lies behind it all. On the other side of that lies his resurrection, which is a sign of God's power. Thus in his comparison with the super-apostles, Paul turns the question about weakness and strength completely upside down. It is *precisely* in his weakness (of which the opponents had made so much) that his real strength is to be found. "For whenever I am weak, then I am strong" (12:10, see in **T6.16**). That constitutes his Christ identity. Paul thus builds up a *persona* of himself as an apostle who—in complete contrast to his opponents—is *suffering* on behalf of his message and for that reason precisely living in accordance with the message itself. In this, so the Corinthians must understand, he is a model for their own identity as Christ believers, showing them how they themselves should be.

Could Paul expect the Corinthians to understand and be convinced by an argument as convoluted as this? At least, he did not! For he concludes the whole letter rather more firmly (12:19–21; 13:2–4, 10):

> **T6.18** [12:19]Have you been thinking all along that we have been defending ourselves before you? (No:) we are speaking in Christ before God. Everything we do, beloved, is for the sake of building you up. [20]For I fear that when I come, I may find you not as I wish,

> and that you may find me not as you wish; I fear that there may perhaps be quarreling, jealousy, anger, selfishness, slander, gossip, conceit, and disorder. [21]I fear that when I come again, my God may humble me before you, and that I may have to mourn over many who previously sinned and have not repented of the impurity, sexual immorality, and licentiousness that they have practiced. . . . [13:2]I warned those who sinned previously and all the others, and I warn them now when I am absent, as if I were present on my second visit, that if I come again, I will not be lenient—[3]since you desire proof that Christ is speaking in me. He is not weak in dealing with you, but is powerful in you. [4]For he was crucified in weakness, but lives by the power of God. We, too, are weak in him, but we will live with him by the power of God in relation to you. . . . [10]Therefore, I write these things while I am away from you, so that when I come, I may not have to be severe in using the authority that the Lord has given me, which is for building up and not for tearing down.

In this text, Paul briefly (13:3–4) plays on the weakness of Christ, which is also a power, but that aside, he is not beating about the bush. When he arrives, he will show no mercy if they do not behave. He will not tear them down. That he will only do to the external opponents. But if they do not themselves understand, he must find other, harsher means—but still for their upbuilding (13:10)! Thus Paul ends the whole letter on a much more authoritative tone (see 13:2–3), corresponding to his claim that it is Christ himself who is speaking in him (13:3).

Before turning to the question of the inner connection of the whole of the canonical 2 Corinthians, we may summarize Paul's rhetorical strategy in the second half of the letter (chapters 10–13) as follows. He directly addresses the Corinthians in the second person as if they still belong within the Christ circle even though he has a strong sense that some of them have been attracted by his external opponents, who are clearly outside the circle. He also speaks indirectly in the third person about the same opponents, with whom he does battle quite strongly, and also about those among the Corinthians who may already be on the opponents' side. In his direct address to the Corinthians as a group, he employs a range of rhetorical strategies: there is the usual encouragement, which presupposes that the addressees are within the Christ circle; there is also a more ironical form of address, which remains gentle and is not intended to push the addressees into the fold of the opponents. In the same direct address to the Corinthians, he also engages in a piece of genuine self-praise (in comparing himself with his opponents), which he turns around so that it becomes a witness to his claim that *only Paul* may in fact boast in Christ. Finally, he ends up not mincing matters in declaring that he will know no mercy when he arrives. This is all directed to the Corinthians as a group but of course not least to those among them who risk going astray. Even here, however, it seems presupposed that the addressees will fall into line when their merciless apostle turns up. Putting it all together, it makes excellent sense to see Paul's overall strategy in the whole of 2 Corinthians 10–13 as closely reflecting his question to them in the previous letter, 1 Corinthians 4:21:

> (**T6.9**) 21What would you prefer? Am I to come to you with a stick, or with love in a pneuma of gentleness?

We should conclude that even though Paul is much more concerned about the Corinthians in the second letter than in the first, and much more direct in his confrontation with his external opponents, his basic rhetorical strategy remains integrative, aiming at inclusion of as many among the Corinthians as possible. His almost tortured development of his own *persona* as their suffering apostle of Christ serves the same aim. Those he attacks (but in the third person) in the middle section (10:12–12:10; see, e.g., **T6:13**) are his direct opponents.

PAUL'S STRATEGY IN 2 CORINTHIANS 1–7 AND 10–13

As noted, scholars have felt that Paul's tone of voice is so different in 2 Corinthians 1–7 and 10–13 that these two parts of the transmitted canonical letter must be or belong to two different letters. In chapters 1–7, he is confident and rejoices at the Corinthians; in chapters 10–13, he threatens them that he will be merciless on his arrival. Will that cohere?

The answer is yes—as soon as one sees the subtlety of Paul's rhetorical strategy. It is true that he declares in 2 Corinthians 7 that he is full of confidence concerning the Corinthians (7:16):

> **(T5.32)** 16*I rejoice,* in that I may have complete confidence in you.

But this is far from all he is doing. On the contrary, as we saw, he has spelled out to them the psychodrama that he had ostensibly undergone on the way from Ephesus to Macedonia, and he now sends this account to the Corinthians as the strongest possible reminder of *how* worried their apostle was on their behalf! This can only be explained in one way: Paul was in fact *not* certain that he could trust the Corinthians in everything. If one understands his account of the psychodrama in this way, it makes excellent sense that he should have conceived the two letter halves as part of a single letter. In the first half, he presents a very strongly phrased renewed appeal to the Corinthians, one that reflects his continued concern about them and constitutes a sustained defense of his own relations with them. Once that has been established, he engages, in the second half, in a much more explicit (if still indirect) confrontation of his opponents—but for the same purpose of integrating the Corinthians with himself, including those who had been attracted by the opponents. Thus understood, the whole letter hangs closely together.

That Paul did *not* feel confident about the Corinthians is clear already from the first letter half, in spite of the fact that in chapter 7

(7:5–16), he celebrates his joy at having received good news about them from Titus. The apex of the psychodrama described in 2 Corinthians 2:14–7:4 is an account of Paul's *persona* as an apostle of God. We should not take this as a kind of general account with no immediate rhetorical function. On the contrary, it is addressed directly to the Corinthians and ends with a number of imperatives with an immense linguistic power. What we see here is the way Paul uses language with an intensity without equal in an attempt to build up his own *persona*—and as always in relation to his immediate addressees. We have already met parts of the text (see **T5.30**). However, in order to get a sense of who Paul was, both in his rhetorical *persona* and most likely also in his personal self-understanding, one must have the whole text in front of one. Fortunately, at this point, the reader of this book will be able to follow the apostle the way he intended. Here is the text (2 Cor 5:20–6:13; 7:2–4):

> **T6.19** [5:20]So we [Paul himself] are ambassadors for Christ, since God is making his appeal through us; we entreat you on behalf of Christ: be reconciled to God. [21]For our sake he [God] made him [Christ] to be sin who knew no sin, so that in him we might become the righteousness of God. [6:1]As we work together with him, we urge you also not to accept the grace of God in vain. [2]For it says, "At an acceptable time I have listened to you, and on a day of salvation I have helped you." See, now is the acceptable time; see, now is the day of salvation! [3]We are putting no obstacle in anyone's way, so that no fault may be found with our ministry, [4]but as servants of God we have commended ourselves in every way: [1] through great endurance, in afflictions, hardships, calamities, [5]beatings, imprisonments, riots, labors, sleepless nights, hunger; [6][2] by purity, knowledge, patience, kindness, holiness of pneuma, genuine love, [7]truthful speech, and the power of God; [3] with the weapons of righteousness for the right hand and for the left; [8]in honor and dishonor, in ill repute and good repute; as impostors, and

> yet true; [9]as unknown, and yet well known; as dying, and look—we are alive; as punished, and yet not killed; [10]as sorrowful, yet always rejoicing; as poor, yet making many rich; as having nothing, and yet possessing everything—: [11]our mouth is wide open toward you, Corinthians, our heart is spread out (to you). [12]There is no narrow room in us, but you have narrow room in your own interior. [13]In return—I speak as to children—open wide your hearts also. . . . [7:2]Make room in your hearts for us; we have wronged no one, we have corrupted no one, we have taken advantage of no one. [3]I do not say this to condemn you, for I said before that you are in our hearts, to die together and to live together. [4]I often boast about you; I have great pride in you; I am filled with encouragement; I am overjoyed in all our affliction.

The end of this text (7:4) leads directly into Paul's account of his joy when Titus returned with good news from Corinth. But what has Paul been saying before that? He has presented himself as a messenger coming directly from God and Christ (5:20–6:2). Then he has described the concrete form that his service takes (6:3–10). In this, he lists first ([1], 6:4–5) a number of afflictions; next ([2], 6:6–7) an ascending number of inner attitudes through which he conquers all the afflictions; then ([3], 6:7–8) a set of positive and negative external circumstances in which his inner attitudes come to expression; and finally (again [3], 6:8–10) descriptions of the apostles (i.e., Paul himself!) that mention, first, how they are ordinarily understood by people and, second, how they should *rightly* be understood. Here, too, he presents an ascending line that ends like this: "as having nothing [so people say], and yet possessing *everything* [in actual fact]." In summary, Paul has led his reader through a story that tells of this: (1) external afflictions, (2) the inner basis for handling the afflictions, and finally (3) the apostle's concrete appearance in confronting the people who stand behind the afflictions. The idea behind this story is that the confrontations lead to afflictions, *but* the afflictions are conquered by the apostle on the basis of his inner attitudes. That is the core of the *persona* Paul builds up rhetorically as a model for his addressees.

Could he have stopped here? Perhaps. But he doesn't! The whole long account given in 6:3–10 leads directly into what is its conclusion: Paul's mouth is open toward the Corinthians and his heart is spread out to them (6:11). Thus the account is directed toward the imperatives telling them that they, on their side, must spread themselves out to Paul (6:13) and contain him (7:2), just as he, on his side, is spread out to them and has his mouth open toward them (6:11).

What is Paul talking about in all this? There is only one possible answer: community. Paul says, calls, indeed shouts to the Corinthians that they must share with him in handling all external circumstances and situations—circumstances that are in reality wholly unimportant, since they do not touch the fact that through God's power (6:7, the final point in *that* line), Christ believers possess *everything* (6:10, the final point in *that* line). We know from chapter 7 of the letter that the Corinthians had responded positively to Titus's visit. But Paul did not in the end feel confident about this. That is why he *in the letter itself* spells out once again his call to them with all the power of his language. Spelling out his call in this particular way is the whole point of the story Paul has constructed of the psychodrama he underwent on his way across the Hellespont.

The reader must not necessarily like the character of Paul's appeal. But think about it as something Paul has dictated and sent to the congregation in Corinth. Did he know no limits? He was at least himself wholly fixated on Christ, and he wanted others to be the same. Within that framework, one cannot get around the fact that here is a man who was able to communicate. It is all immensely alive.

We should conclude that there is no reason for dividing up 2 Corinthians into two or more original letters. It all hangs together, guided by the apostle's *continued* concern about the Corinthians.

We should also conclude that in Paul, we from time to time find a complete match between his message and his manner of communicating it. **T6.19** is an especially good example. In this text, Paul conjures up his own apostolic *persona* in a manner that in itself directly reflects his message (he almost behaves like Christ himself) and also—in the way he presents it (his openness toward others)—addresses the Corinthians in a similar manner. Here Paul's rhetorical practice directly and powerfully matches his message.

PAUL'S PERSONA AND IDENTITY

We have considered a number of examples of the way Paul in his letters creates a special *persona* and identity for himself. The examples most often turn up where he was under pressure, either directly from opponents or from undecided Christ believers in the congregations he had himself founded. This happens in Galatians, both at the beginning (1:1–5 [**T5.5**]; 1:6–9 [**T3.1**]) and the end (6:12–15 [**T0.6**]; 6:17–18 [**T0.7**]). It in fact also happens in 1 Corinthians (4:6–13 [**T6.8**]) and especially in the central parts of 2 Corinthians, not least 5:20–6:13 and 7:2–4 (**T6.19**). The *persona* that Paul here creates is that of an apostle who is in complete conformity with Christ himself. This *persona* is, on the one hand, wholly independent of all others in that he has been sent directly by God. By separating himself from the recipients of his letter, he also behaves in a way that is potentially exclusive. However, we have also seen that precisely when he is in conformity with Christ, Paul also behaves in a manner that is strongly integrative, thereby reflecting the very *content* of that conformity. In his rhetorical practice, he basically intends to create the community of love that constitutes the core of his message.

I said that the *persona* that Paul constructs for himself is a tragic figure. There are two closely connected reasons for this. First, it contains a central duality between being, on the one hand, completely self-reliant (based on Christ and God) and being, on the other hand, to an extreme degree open toward the Christ believers in Paul's own congregations. Second, precisely in this openness, it is also *dependent* on others. In a way, Paul can do nothing about his relationship with his congregations. *Everything* depends on *them*—namely, how they will respond. And yet in his letters, he precisely attempts—and with all the means at his disposal—to make that crucial difference. That is what gives them their enormous intensity. And that is also what gives them a character that is—at least potentially—tragic. What if in spite of all his efforts they did *not* understand and accept what he was saying?

We, on our side, may console the apostle with the fact that his letters and the *persona* he developed in them for quite specific purposes have made a colossal impact *after* his death. That is something after all.

* * *

Our task in this chapter has been to investigate Paul's rhetorical practice where he was bent on generating exclusion. However, we have seen that genuine exclusion only comes up in connection with the apostle's direct opponents. I wish they would castrate themselves! They are Satan's brood! But then these unhappy people are not the direct addressees of the letters. With regard to those among the addressees whom we called the undecided, we have seen that Paul in fact continued to speak in integrative ways. And I ended up suggesting that in his aim to include *all*, Paul went so far in his rhetorical *persona* as to expose himself completely, with a potential tragedy as the consequence.

How should we ourselves react to all this? We must at least recognize the power and intensity of it all. We should also permit ourselves to admire the degree of match we have seen between Paul's community-creating practice and the basis for and ultimate goal of that practice: that the addressees and Paul himself live together in the kind of community that it was the whole point of Christ to establish, the only one that Paul took to be good. In addition, we should acknowledge that in the way Paul articulates the content of the Christ community in his maxim and his lists of the proper attitudes, it *is* good; compare the attitudes he mentions in 2 Corinthians 6:6–7 (see in **T6.19**): magnanimity, goodness, genuine love. When we hear about these attitudes, we may well ask our fellow human beings, Are you against them or perhaps just not concerned about them? If in either respect the answer is yes, then there is little to be done about it.

Finally, we may feel joy when somebody is able to write in such a manner that there is a *persona* here who is wholly alive, even after two thousand years. We don't really care about history, not even our own. Don't we care, either, about other people who are genuinely capable? Paul shows us what we will in that case lose.

CONCLUSION

PAUL AND IDENTITY POLITICS

IN THIS CONCLUSION, I will do two things: first, summarize what has been said throughout the book about Paul's understanding of the identity of Christ believers, and next, attempt to show that this is all not only interesting in itself but also of direct relevance to us. Until now, we have aimed to be loyal to Paul's own ways of thinking, and we will continue to be so in the summary. When we then take the huge step in the direction of discussing certain current issues concerning national identity, identity politics, and democracy in the West, it is clear that we must put quite important parts of Paul's thought behind us. However, we will also see that the precise ideas in Paul that we can in fact employ are not just peripheral to his thought. In fact, they are quite central, as will be clear in the summary.

SUMMARY ON PAUL: MESSIANISM AND ETHICS, THE DOUBLE MODEL OF IDENTITY, RHETORICAL PRACTICE

In chapters 1 and 2, we saw how, according to Paul, God has acted and will act to make human beings righteous. He sent Christ in the figure of Jesus to die and be resurrected and to appear once again very soon on the day of judgment. He also effected the consequences of this for human beings, in both the present after the death and resurrection of Jesus Christ and at his return. They have responded (some of them!) with faithfulness, thereby becoming righteous (even sinless) so that they, too, will be resurrected on the day of judgment to be together with Christ. We also saw that the key to this effect on human beings was that in being vertically directed toward God through Christ (in "Christ faith"), they would also be directed horizontally toward one another in genuine love as expressed in what I called Paul's maxim (see in **T2.5**). In addition, we saw that a key element in bringing about this consequence was the pneuma. It was crucially present not only in the story of the resurrection of Christ (in the past) and of believers (in the future) but also in the ethical life of believers in the present once they, too, have had their Christ faith confirmed by receiving the pneuma in baptism.

All of this constitutes Paul's central story about Jesus Christ. As is already clear, it has direct implications for the manner of life here and now of the Christ believers whom he is addressing. When they live "in a manner worthy of the gospel of Christ" (Phil 1:27), which they both must and will do, they will concretely look "*not* to your own interests, *but* to the interests of others" (Phil 2:4, see in **T2.5**). That—as captured in the notion of having "(Christ) faith (that is) working through love" (Gal 5:6, see **T2.1** below)—is what constitutes the essential identity of Christ believers.

However, that is not all there is to be said of their identity. For they also are and continue to be either Jews or non-Jews, masters or slaves, men or women (and many more things in addition). How, then, do these diverse identities fit with the single identity that they all share? In chapters 3 and 4, we addressed this issue. This is where we introduced the Pauline "double model" that serves to answer that question. It is articulated, for instance, in the crucial verse Galatians 5:6:

> (**T2.1**) [6]For in Christ Jesus neither circumcision nor uncircumcision counts for anything; the only thing that counts is faith working through love.

What this verse means is that "in Christ Jesus," being a Jew or a non-Jew does not *matter* at all for what Paul has spoken about in the immediately preceding verse: righteousness (and hence salvation). Only one thing matters: Christ faith working through love. However, this does not mean, of course, that *being* a Jew or a non-Jew has suddenly disappeared. Christ believers both are and continue to be either Jews or non-Jews (and insofar as they are the latter, also Greeks, Romans, Scythians, etc.). As we just noted, Paul connects the one thing that they *all* are and have in common—in the one identity that genuinely matters—with the pneuma. Thus we may also say that Paul's double model is a model of pneuma, on the one hand, and "flesh," or sarx, on the other. "Pneumatically," Christ believers are all one; in the flesh, or "sarkically," they will also differ.

However, it is important to notice that this idea is not at all captured by merely saying that believers are identical "spiritually" while of course also different in actual fact. For their being identical "pneumatically" is just as much an actual fact as their being different in the flesh. As we saw, in Paul's conception (and he employed himself as an example), they are already now being materially *suffused* with pneuma, which is already now *changing* their bodies of flesh and blood. And so we need a more satisfactory understanding precisely of the relationship between these two features: a "pneumatic" identity and a number of "sarkic" differences.

To get this, we spelled out in chapters 3–4 Paul's double model in two respects. First, in accordance with the understanding in Stoicism of what is a closely related model, we said that while the "sarkic" differences were completely "indifferent" (Greek *adiaphora*) in relation to the one thing that matters at the top level (in Paul, righteousness and salvation; in Stoicism, the good), nevertheless the various things at the lower level were not in themselves entirely worthless. They might well be allowed to play *some* role in the perception of one's identity and for one's behavior as long as they did not interfere with the only thing that genuinely mattered.

Second, in Paul, this very specific relationship between the two levels was *grounded* in his perception of the one thing that mattered at the top level as expressed in his maxim of love. People were allowed to have their diverse identities at the lower level *by the fact that* the only thing that genuinely mattered to all of them was that each individual would only be concerned for *the others* (which includes a perception of their various identities) and not for themselves. In this way, Paul managed to hold the two levels very tightly together. What he has placed at the top level (namely, totally other-regarding love) *grounds* that the things that belong at the lower level may retain *some* importance. But there are two conditions for this. First, the things at the lower level must not interfere with the one thing at the top level. Second, the beneficiaries of such love must themselves return it to the others with similar consequences for *them*.

In chapters 3 and 4, we saw how Paul employed this—as I believe—very powerful model in what he says about Jews and non-Jews in Christ, about masters and slaves in Christ, and about men and women in Christ. We also considered Paul's attitude toward some other "sarkic" facts: sex and the relationship of Christ believers to the worldly powers. In both cases, Paul's specific recommendations can be seen to rely on the double model of pneuma and sarx in the form we have just seen.

Finally, in chapters 5 and 6, we addressed the question of how Paul's understanding of his basic Christ message, as we had spelled this out in the previous four chapters, was also played out in his own rhetorical practice: his way of addressing those to whom he was writing. What we saw was a striking use of the double model itself. On the one hand, he insists—as a genuine "faith fanatic"—on Christ faith as the only thing that matters. On the other hand, the double model also allowed Paul to be much more differentiated and in fact open-minded in his rhetorical practice in relation to all the *differences* that continue to mark even Christ believers. We saw how this open-mindedness on Paul's part directly reflected his understanding of the central Christ message and how we may therefore say that Paul applied his own understanding of how others should live in accordance with the Christ gospel to himself and his own rhetorical practice toward them. Without wishing in any way to praise Paul unduly, I claimed that this practice is in fact quite moving. When are we ourselves able to do the same?

In pursuing this agenda, we spent some time analyzing Paul's various rhetorical tools for generating what he was ultimately after: inclusion and harmony in the Christ community. We also went into some detail on two letters where Paul is at his most confrontational: Galatians and 2 Corinthians. What we saw was that although he was here working toward exclusion, his attempt to generate inclusion gained the upper hand even here. Those to be excluded were his direct opponents, whom he did not directly address in those letters but only spoke about in the third-person singular or plural. By contrast, those he directly addressed in the second-person plural were meant to be included with Paul himself in the Christ community for which he was working. To them, therefore, he constantly appealed, arguing his case as best he could in order to let them see what he took to be the truth. One important result of this analysis was that in this particular dimension of Paul's rhetoric, which is central to the letters, there was not in fact any great difference between 1 and 2 Corinthians—against what many scholars have thought. In both letters, Paul is basically arguing for inclusion.

Let me add this new point. I hope that the reader of this book has obtained a strong sense of the incredible richness of Paul's writing as he presents and develops the themes we have followed in chapters 1–2, 3–4, and 5–6. This richness reflects what I take to be a chronological development in the letters that has a special character. It seems that as the letters progressed in time, Paul spent more and more time spelling out (quasi-)*philosophically* what it all meant and how the various elements in his message cohered. In this development from the earliest letter, 1 Thessalonians, to the last, Romans, I believe we can detect how Greco-Roman philosophy helped Paul articulate his message more thoroughly as he was confronted—for instance, in Galatians and 1 Corinthians—with issues that called for all his inventiveness. I also suggest that this added philosophical dimension in the letters lies behind the refinements of Paul's rhetorical practice that we studied in chapters 5–6. However, even as enriched with philosophy, the mind and the voice are throughout uniquely Paul's own.

FROM PAUL TO US

In the second half of this conclusion, I will attempt to do what a number of European philosophers have been doing during the last thirty years: employ Paul to give input into a modern political discussion. These philosophers include, for instance, the French philosopher Alain Badiou (born 1937) and the Italian political theorist and philosopher Giorgio Agamben (born 1942). In various books from around the turn of the millennium, they have focused on some specific ideas in Paul that they have developed in a modern context. In the case of Badiou, the core text is Galatians 3:26–28:

> (**T0.14**) [26]For in Christ Jesus you are all sons of God through faith. [27]As many of you as were baptized into Christ have clothed yourselves with Christ. [28]There is *no longer Jew or Greek*, there is *no longer slave or free*, there is *no longer male and female*; for *all of you are one in Christ Jesus.*

As we noted in the introduction, Badiou took this to mean that Paul spoke of a form of universalism.

In the case of Agamben, the core text is 1 Corinthians 7:29–31:

> (**T4.3**) [29]What I mean, brothers, is this: the appointed time has grown short; from now on, let even those who have wives be as if they had none, [30]and those who mourn as if they were not mourning, and those who rejoice as if they were not rejoicing, and those who

> buy as if they had no possessions, [31]and those who deal with the world as if they had no dealings with it. For the form of this world is passing away.

Agamben took this text to express particularly clearly Paul's eschatological messianism. He is certainly right here, but how that idea should be translated into a modern political context is something one must read in Agamben himself. His attempt is fascinating (in a tradition that goes back, among others, to the German thinker Walter Benjamin) but also (to my less "continental" mind) somewhat opaque.

More directly relevant is Badiou's presentation of Paul as the "founder of universalism." Here Badiou primarily focuses on the highest level in what I have called Paul's double model where all Christ believers share a single thing, which is the community in Christ. This focus is of course entirely right, but we already know that it is also too one-sided. In Paul himself, Christ believers both share a single Christ identity and may also have various other identities at a lower level. The latter need to be brought in too. For they *are* there, and they remain there. Indeed, as we will see, it is precisely this Pauline double perspective on identity that is relevant to us.

We will consider all this toward the end of this conclusion. Before that, I will lay the groundwork by looking at the modern political issues themselves. Here I will draw on two political scientists in the United States: Francis Fukuyama (Stanford University), particularly in his recent book *Identity: The Demand for Dignity and the Politics of Resentment* (2018), and Deborah Schildkraut (Tufts University) in a survey essay on "National Identity in the United States" (2011; see the literature section at the end of the book). Our topic will be a single, precisely defined one—namely, the relationship between identity politics and a sense of national identity. Thus we will of course not address all the current problems in democracies in the West. As a case study, we will be looking at our specific topic in relation to the United States. Once we have seen the problem to be solved in this field, we will consider how Paul's ideas may contribute to the solution.

THE MODERN PROBLEM: THE RELATIONSHIP BETWEEN IDENTITY POLITICS AND NATIONAL IDENTITY IN LIBERAL DEMOCRACIES

An urgent problem at present in liberal democracies in the West is how to find room for various forms of identity politics within those democracies when they should also continue to be built around a reasonably strong sense of national identity. The latter will have to be shared by all and so requires some degree of uniformity. By contrast, the former will by definition focus on particular groups as different from others and so will generate a strong sense of diversity. How may the two positions be held together? Superficially, at least, they seem to be moving in opposite directions—one toward uniformity, the other toward diversity.

The question has become urgent over the last few decades, not least due to the arrival in many countries of immigrants with a number of different cultural backgrounds. But it is also a question that has become pervasive internally to each country in the wake of a growing individualism in the Western world that has its roots back in the Enlightenment and even further back. At present, identity politics covers not only Blacks and Latinos (in the United States) and Arabic Muslims (in Europe) but also women, people with non-binary sexual orientations, people with physical disabilities, and so on. In the current political fights around these issues in liberal democracies in North America and Europe, the basic features that have created the liberal democracies begin to be jeopardized. The fights put the sense of a shared national identity that should support these democracies at risk.

In the book mentioned, Francis Fukuyama argues for two propositions in relation to this overall issue with which we should strongly agree. One is that there is in fact a need in liberal democracies for a reasonably strong sense of national identity. Fukuyama lists a number of things that such a sense may deliver. There is physical security. There is good government. There is an ability to facilitate economic development. There is an ability to promote a wide radius of trust. Finally, there is an ability to maintain strong social security nets that mitigate economic inequality. These things may come about when, as a result of deliberation and debate, citizens are prepared to accept outcomes that they do not themselves like or prefer in the interest of the common good. As Fukuyama says, "A culture of tolerance and mutual sympathy must override partisan passions" (p. 131). That is what a clear sense of national identity will provide.

The other proposition for which Fukuyama argues—and again rightly—is the legitimacy of the identity political urge itself. The agendas for which the civil rights movement and the women's movement were fighting in the United States from around the 1950s onward were entirely justified and can be directly derived from the liberal ideas underlying the Constitution of the United States, including those of freedom and equality. There is a risk here, as Fukuyama also shows, of identical political focus groups proliferating interminably, basing themselves on the idea that they alone know and understand from personal experience the amount of repression from which they are suffering. But the fact remains that all citizens in a liberal democracy do have a right to claim to be fully recognized for who they are as part of such a society.

How, then, should the two propositions be combined? Can we find a way of securing a reasonably strong sense of national identity shared by all—at the same time as we also make room for the identity claims of individual groups? To achieve this, Fukuyama makes two moves that in themselves bring us quite close to Paul. At the same time, he also leaves us with a problem. And here, as we will see, Paul has a solution that is, I believe, stronger than anything to be found in Fukuyama.

For one thing, Fukuyama claims that an adequate national identity must be, as he dubs it, "creedal." It must not, for instance, be based on geography (Latin *ius soli*, "the right of the soil") or on ethnicity (Latin *ius sanguinis*, "the right of blood") in an old-fashioned "blood and soil" nationalism. Instead, it must consist in a set of higher-order ways of understanding a national identity that together have the same obligatory character as a religious confession or creed. In America, this is reflected in what kids in the American school system are expected to learn about the nation's past (including the Constitution), in the naturalization oath of allegiance to the United States of America that new citizens must swear, in the Pledge of Allegiance to stars and stripes, and the like. In this respect, as Fukuyama rightly claims, the United States is well ahead of many countries in Europe, where the sense of national identity is in one way or the other tied to "blood and soil." It goes without saying that for the purpose of showing the relevance of Paul to these considerations, the fact that the required national identity must be creedal fits in exceedingly well. For Pauline Christ faith is "creedal" throughout.

Fukuyama's second move is to work on the two notions of assimilation and integration. Here he is in wider company with other political scientists. Assimilation is the idea of one minority group adopting the values of the dominant or "core" group in society and at the same time leaving their own original values behind. This idea lies behind the notion of the American "melting pot," which was articulated by writer Israel Zangwill in a play with the same title from 1908 and continued to be powerful in the American imagination well up into the twentieth century. Integration draws on a different notion of "cultural pluralism," which was introduced in 1924 by philosopher Horace Kallen and eventually turned into "multiculturalism." Here the idea is that the minority groups retain a significant portion of their cultural origin at the same time as they are also participating in the dominant culture. Instead of speaking of a "melting pot," other metaphors have been used: a "salad bowl" or a "mosaic." This fits Fukuyama's own proposal that in incorporating minority groups into the national identity, one must *redefine* the national identity so as to make it inclusive and capable of genuinely honoring the diverse reality of the society in question.

Fukuyama's understanding of the character of national identity and integration that is required appears to be in principle right. At the same time, if the national identity must be creedal and if it must be redefined for purposes of inclusion so as to make room for the actual diversity in society, the question arises with some force what this national identity will actually consist in and look like. How will it concretely fulfill the requirement for inclusion? Fukuyama unfortunately does not address this question. This is where Paul will be of help.

To see the problem in its full size and also to get some indication of what should go into a renewed definition of American national identity, we may draw on Deborah Schildkraut's research in the survey essay mentioned from 2011. The data for that survey goes back to 2004. Things may of course have changed since then, but hopefully not to an extent that should seriously worry us here. What Schildkraut is after is the understanding of American national identity that a representative cross section of American citizens had at the time. She collected the various options under four rubrics: Liberalism, Civic republicanism, Ethnoculturalism, and Incorporationism. These evidently need to be defined, but Schildkraut does not spend too much time on that, choosing instead to let them be defined by the various items that she subsumes under either. And these are what we are after. Where the four rubrics are somewhat abstract categories employed by political and other scientists for their own purposes, the items that belong under them are much closer to what Americans themselves consider to be a salient part of what it is to be an American.

Under *Liberalism* (which she has previously outlined in terms of "freedom, equality, opportunity, rule of law, and minimal government intervention into the private lives of citizens," p. 858), Schildkraut places these items:

1. Respecting America's political institutions and laws
2. Pursuing economic success through hard work
3. Letting other people say what they want, no matter how much you disagree with them

Under *Civic republicanism* (which one may define as a type of political thought that emphasizes the interaction between individual freedom and civic participation in political life aiming at the common good), she lists the following items:

4. Doing volunteer work in one's community
5. Thinking of oneself as American
6. Feeling American
7. Being informed about local and national politics
8. Being involved in local and national politics

As may be seen, Liberalism and Civic republicanism to some extent balance one another—Liberalism "from the top down" by emphasizing the freedom of the individual and the equality of all vis-à-vis the ruling authorities and Civic republicanism "from the bottom up" by emphasizing the involvement of individuals in the common good.

Under *Ethnoculturalism* (which is quite close to European "blood and soil" nationalism), Schildkraut lists the following items:

9. Being born in America
10. Being a Christian
11. Having European ancestors
12. Being white

By contrast, *Incorporationism* (a type of political thought that allows citizens to celebrate their ethnic heritage at the same time as they are also being integrated into the country's dominant culture) has the following items:

13. Carrying on the cultural traditions of one's ancestors, such as language and food
14. Respecting other people's cultural differences
15. Blending into the larger society
16. Seeing people of all backgrounds as American

Clearly, these two groups are directly opposed to one another. Together, they reflect the current urgent issue in the United States (also seen in several European countries): What should count as the national identity in the face of the actual diversity in these countries as reflected in the various identity political movements that emphasize diversity over uniformity?

What Schildkraut did was to ask her select group of informants whether any of the features she has listed is "very important" or "somewhat important" for defining what it is to be an American. The result is fascinating. Some items come out with a very high backing (80–90 percent or more)—for example, items 1–7. Others have a fairly low backing, particularly the ethnoculturalist items, with item 12, being white, as the lowest (10 percent). (One wonders, though, what the percentage of this item would be in the 2020s.) The last four items under Incorporationism are particularly revealing. While items 14 and 16 on respecting others and so on have a very high backing (over 90 percent in all), items 13 and 15 on carrying on one's own cultural practices versus blending into the larger society both have a high backing of around 75 percent when one adds together "very important" and "somewhat important," but here there is an almost equal distinction between these two ratings. Only about one-third of the respondents consider item 13 on carrying on one's own cultural practices to be "*very* important." And only one-third consider item 15 on blending to be "*very* important."

Schildkraut's survey helps us fill in much more concretely what should go into Fukuyama's creedal understanding of American national identity. At the same time, it also points very clearly to *the* fundamental question that we are after: an unresolved relationship between identity politics (as reflected in item 13—carrying on the cultural traditions of one's ancestors) and an idea of uniformity (item 15—blending into the larger society), which issues in unease and some disagreement whether one thing or the other is *very* important. Interestingly, however, the survey also shows that there is a very high level of agreement (over 90 percent) on items 14, respecting other people's cultural differences, and 16, seeing people of all backgrounds as American.

How is Paul relevant to all that?

THE PAULINE SOLUTION

What we need in order to resolve the tension revealed in Schildkraut's survey is a way of combining a concern for the "larger" or "dominant" or "core" society with an emphasis on cultural diversity. That is, we need to find a way of overcoming the opposition inherent in Schildkraut's item 15, blending into the larger society, and her item 13, carrying on the cultural traditions of one's ancestors. Even if Incorporationism is itself defined as containing both, we need to see how it *can* do that when the two items are also superficially opposed to one another, as the backing of either shows. This will also be along the lines of Fukuyama's suggestion that the overall national identity must be redefined for the purpose of generating a genuine form of integration that safeguards and celebrates minority groups' retaining a significant portion of their cultural distinctiveness. How can that aim in fact be fulfilled?

Curiously, the very high level of agreement we just noted among Americans on Schildkraut's items 14 and 16 points in the Pauline direction. What these two items share is a willingness to let other people be the way *they* want to be. This is exactly the content of the ethical dimension of Pauline Christ faith that is captured in the two phrases of "faith(fulness) that is active through love" (Gal 5:6, **T2.1**) and looking "*not* to your own interests, *but* to the interests of others" (Phil 2:4, see in **T2.5**). Moreover, we have seen that in Paul, this conception of the single uniform value shared by all Christ believers at the top level of his double model directly *grounds* the legitimacy of a concern for diversity at the lower level. Thus by bringing in Paul's double model with the specific content that it has at the top level, we may manage to resolve the tension between items 13 and 15 in Schildkraut's survey and to honor Fukuyama's call for a redefinition of American national identity that will make genuine room for cultural diversity in a precise and coherent way.

What I am proposing here is that once we have carefully considered what these two modern political scientists have to say about identity issues in modern liberal democracies, we can see that a model developed by Paul for handling similar issues in his own congregations may be used to solve a current problem. In itself, this is perhaps not so surprising. After all, many of the items in Schildkraut's list of what it is to be an American go back not only to the Enlightenment but through that route also to certain central Christian ideas that were precisely secularized in the Enlightenment. It remains the case that the Pauline model of a completely altruistic love at the top level and a legitimate concern for specificity at the lower level may illuminate from within the interconnection between the various items that go into a modern understanding of American national identity. Not only that: it may solve a question that was left over in both Fukuyama and Schildkraut. At the same time, it may also sharpen our understanding of what is fundamentally at stake in those various items.

Here is what this means. Think of the American national identity as consisting, to begin with, of what lies at the top level in Paul's double model: look "*not* to your own interests, *but* to the interests of others." What this will give us are, in the first place, Schildkraut's items 14 and 16. They are in themselves a direct expression of the Pauline maxim when this is applied to the actual fact of cultural diversity in society. But the Pauline principle will also give us a fair amount of the items that fall under Liberalism and Civic republicanism. Underlying item 1 on respecting the rule of law lies a sense of equality among all citizens that may itself be derived from the Pauline maxim. Similarly, item 3 on freedom of speech is an immediate expression of the maxim in one specific area. Items 4–8 under Civic republicanism may also be derived from it. They all draw on the basic idea of the individual working for the common good. Note, however, that the common good must here be understood not just as consisting in what everybody will agree on. Instead, due to the radical character of the Pauline maxim, it will consist in precisely the kind of community that is established once people act on the Pauline maxim, a community in which everyone is constantly both listening and bowing to the views of the others.

What cannot be derived from the maxim are the ethnoculturalist items 9–12, even item 10 on being a Christian. For as these appear in Schildkraut's survey, they are in their exclusivity directly opposed to the Pauline maxim. They all focus on *one* set of "sarkic" differences from others in the mix of actual diversity in society and insist on elevating *that* to the top level. Sometimes they even elevate that same set of differences into having universal status, which is one risk in the "universalism" celebrated by Alain Badiou. However, that goes wholly against the Pauline principle. (Indeed, here modern American ethnoculturalists, as defined by items 9–12, in fact shake hands with Paul's Jewish opponents in Galatians.) By contrast, were one—as a white Christian born in America but with European ancestors—to accept the Pauline principle at the top, there would be plenty of room at the *lower* level of the double model for precisely those values. But then that would depend on one's also accepting *others* at the same level with the same degree of legitimacy.

Finally, there are Schildkraut's items 13 and 15 on carrying on the cultural traditions of one's ancestors versus blending into the larger society. We noted that as they appear in the survey, these two items are in principle opposed to one another but also that as part of Incorporationism, there should in some way be room for both. Seen in that light, the beautiful thing about Paul's double model is that it is precisely able to include both at the same time. It does so, however, by also qualifying them. If one places Paul's maxim at the top of the double model, one will have created an entity that functions like the "larger society" in item 15. This is what *defines* that society and where *all* members of it therefore belong. By this move, the idea of the "larger society" is fairly radically qualified and redefined from any current candidates. However, since Paul's maxim also allows for diversity and difference, there will also be room at the *lower* level for item 13, not only for those who have hitherto constituted a minority group in society, but also for those who have constituted the majority group as identified in items 9–12. They all have a legitimate and equal place within society as long as they grant the same to all others. This move, then, also *qualifies* the role of the distinctiveness that has hitherto characterized the diverse groups in society. To the extent that they have so far adopted an identity political stance of only fighting for themselves, they will now have achieved the kind of recognition they were fighting for by *giving* the same recognition to others and by seeing their *overall* identity—namely, the *national* one—*elsewhere*: in the principle that then also turns back and fully allows them to keep and celebrate their own specific cultural identity. This identity will evidently continue to be important to them, but its importance will be qualified, since they now *also* see themselves as part of the larger society as defined by the Pauline maxim.

What is particularly beautiful, however, about applying the Pauline model is that it holds the two levels tightly together, since (as we have seen) what is placed at the top level (the national identity) logically *grounds* the legitimacy of what is placed at the lower level (the various diverse identities). That is where applying the Pauline model genuinely solves a problem that was left over in both Fukuyama and Schildkraut. We now have not just the idea of "redefining the national identity so as to make it able to provide integration" (but how?) or the notion of "blending into the larger society" in some unexplained combination with that of "carrying on the cultural traditions of one's ancestors" (or possibly in *opposition* to it?). Instead, what we have is an understanding of the top level, which logically *grounds* precisely the items that are then enabled to flourish at the lower level as long as and inasmuch as these are also qualified by the top value.

I personally find that this whole conception helps us get a better understanding of the concept of the "larger," "dominant," or "core" society that plays such an important role in identity political reflections. "Larger" it will certainly be, since it will be participated in by *all* if *all* were to adopt Paul's maxim as what constitutes the top level of a double model of national identity along Pauline lines. It will certainly also be the "core" society precisely because it is what defines such a society. But "dominant" it will not be. If one adopts Paul's maxim as the key value at the top of society, there will no longer be any group in society that dominates any other. On the contrary, those groups that were previously dominant would see it as their own highest value to consider the interests of *the others*. And conversely. Here there is no domination of anybody by anybody. On the contrary, both minority and majority groups will *all* be logically enabled to have their *own* substantive identities—as it were, as *all* being "minority groups"—*by* the (universal *and* very substantial) identity that they all share at the top level.

All of this may seem quite abstract. And so it is. At the same time, we have also seen how it worked concretely in Paul's handling of a large number of issues in his congregations. At the level of modern political thinking, we may also add that the Pauline picture chimes in well with the idea that a modern liberal democracy is defined not just by everyone's having a free vote but by something much more refined but also concrete: majority concern for minorities—that is, a concern that minority views are respected by the majority and actively *incorporated* into the deepest secret of democracy, which is the *compromise*.

Has an understanding of the American national identity that draws upon Paul's maxim in the way suggested here any future at all? It goes without saying that it was and is an ideal. But as we have previously seen in this book, there is nothing intrinsically wrong with ideals. Ideals are certainly not everything, but we cannot do without them. Let me tell you this personal story. I have up until now spent two full semesters in (and made innumerable visits to) the United States. Whenever I have returned to Denmark, I have had the feeling that political life in Denmark was more "cynical" than in the States, in the sense that the political ideals that *seemed* to underlie the political practice were only very rarely articulated. Conversely, I also felt that in the States, political life was characterized by an unresolved tension between idealism and what one might perhaps call "hypocrisy," where the political ideals were both articulated and not acted on. And so I have thought to myself, How wonderful if we could have a healthy mixture of idealism *and* "cynicism"—that is, of facing the facts about society, including its wild inequalities, and addressing them directly in the light of the idealism! Thus although ideals are certainly not everything, we cannot do without them.

With regard to the practicality of drawing on Paul's maxim in thinking about the American national identity, I have also suggested above that the Pauline maxim may in various ways be seen to underlie large parts of those items that *already* go into what Americans think about their national identity. Indeed, I remember that precisely this was articulated by President John F. Kennedy in his famous inaugural address in January 1961: "Ask not what your country can do for you—ask what you can do for your country." It remains the case that the Pauline maxim is a stark one that only very few among us can in fact fulfill throughout our lives. It therefore needs to be repeated once more here in all its starkness (Phil 2:4, see in **T2.5**):

(**T2.5**) [4]*Let each of you look not to your own interests, but precisely to the interests of others.*

LITERATURE

This list mentions some of the most important books ("classics") that lie behind my own understanding of Paul. For non-experts who want to explore Paul further, I have indicated (with an *) some books that are particularly accessible: short, well written, and the like. (In some cases, one may read the main text and forget about the endnotes.) The list begins with a number of general works on Paul, here mentioned in chronological order, since they indicate a development in Pauline scholarship in the direction of the "new" and then the "radical" perspective on Paul. Then follow some books on the themes addressed in the individual chapters of this book. Finally, I have collected a number of books that address a particular theme that is close to my own heart and underlies everything said in this book without being very explicitly addressed: Paul and philosophy.

GENERAL

Schweitzer, Albert. *The Mysticism of Paul the Apostle*. Baltimore: Johns Hopkins University Press, 1998 (German 1931)—a bold attempt to situate Paul historically in opposition to much traditional, Protestant thinking about the apostle

Munck, Johannes. *Paul and the Salvation of Mankind*. London: SCM, 1959 (German 1954)—another critical account by a Danish scholar that points forward to the later attempt to situate Paul within Judaism

*Stendahl, Krister. *Paul among Jews and Gentiles and Other Essays*. Philadelphia: Fortress, 1976, 133 pp.—a hugely influential, short, and well-written account by a central Swedish scholar

*Dahl, Nils Alstrup. *Studies in Paul: Theology for the Early Christian Mission*. Minneapolis: Augsburg Fortress, 1977, 198 pp.—a crisp and extremely insightful discussion of various Pauline topics by a central Norwegian scholar

Sanders, E. P. *Paul and Palestinian Judaism: A Comparison of Patterns of Religion*. Philadelphia: Fortress, 1977—the founding book for the so-called "new" perspective on Paul and a strong attack on the traditional Protestant understanding of Judaism and Paul's relation to it; not an easy read

———. **Paul, the Law, and the Jewish People*. Philadelphia: Fortress, 1983, 227 pp.—a more easily accessible account that is focused on the central Pauline texts on the topic

———. **Paul*. Past Masters. Oxford: Oxford University Press, 1991, 138 pp.—a magisterial introduction

Holmberg, Bent. *Paul and Power: The Structure of Authority in the Primitive Church as Reflected in the Pauline Epistles*. Coniectanea Biblica, New Testament Series 11. Lund, Sweden: Gleerup, 1978—an early attempt to apply a sociological method to Paul

*Theissen, Gerd. *The Social Setting of Pauline Christianity: Essays on Corinth*. Philadelphia: Fortress, 1982, 210 pp. (German 1974–1975)—a crisp introduction to the social historical and social scientific analysis of Paul

Räisänen, Heikki. *Paul and the Law*. Wissenschaftliche Untersuchungen zum Neuen Testament 29. Tübingen, Germany: Mohr [Siebeck], 1983 (2nd ed., 1987)—a wholly independent account by a leading Finnish scholar, very much in the line of E. P. Sanders

———. *The Rise of Christian Beliefs: The Thought World of Early Christians*. Minneapolis: Fortress, 2010—a magisterial account that situates Paul within early Christianity well into the second century; immensely rewarding, but not an easy read

Meeks, Wayne A. *The First Urban Christians: The Social World of the Apostle Paul*. New Haven, CT: Yale University Press, 1983—a classic, extremely insightful account along social scientific lines; so full that it is not an easy read; compare Still and Horrell below

Segal, Alan F. *Paul the Convert: The Apostolate and Apostasy of Saul the Pharisee*. New Haven, CT: Yale University Press, 1990—one more step toward a Jewish Paul, though still within a "Christian" perspective

Boyarin, Daniel. *A Radical Jew: Paul and the Politics of Identity*. Berkeley: University of California Press, 1994—a brilliant reconstruction of both a Jewish and "Christian" Paul

Stowers, Stanley K. *A Rereading of Romans: Justice, Jews, and Gentiles*. New Haven, CT: Yale University Press, 1994—an innovative and influential reading of the letter to the Romans, in particular, that draws very helpfully on Paul's Greco-Roman context

*Martin, Dale B. *The Corinthian Body*. New Haven, CT: Yale University Press, 1995, 330 pp.—a wonderfully well-written introduction to a modern, anthropologically oriented perspective on Paul; not exactly an easy read but worth the effort

Dunn, James D. G. *The Theology of Paul the Apostle*. Edinburgh: T&T Clark, 1998—a summarizing account from a distinguished scholar who had baptized the "new perspective" on Paul but also understood it along more traditional Protestant lines

Engberg-Pedersen, Troels, ed. *Paul beyond the Judaism/Hellenism Divide*. Louisville, KY: Westminster John Knox, 2001—a collection of essays by an international group of distinguished Pauline scholars who attempt to break down the divide between Judaism and Hellenism in understanding Paul

*Roetzel, Calvin J. *Paul, a Jew on the Margins*. Louisville, KY: Westminster John Knox, 2003, 116 pp.—an insightful introductory account focusing on situating Paul in his cultural context

Watson, Francis. *Paul, Judaism, and the Gentiles: Beyond the New Perspective*. Grand Rapids, MI: Eerdmans, 2007—an extremely insightful mixture of a sociological and a more theological approach to Paul

Still, Todd D., and David G. Horrell, eds. *After the First Urban Christians: The Social-Scientific Study of Pauline Christianity Twenty-Five Years Later*. London: T&T Clark, 2009—an assessment of the continuing importance of Meeks's book (see above)

*Eisenbaum, Pamela. *Paul Was Not a Christian: The Original Message of a Misunderstood Apostle*. New York: HarperCollins, 2009, 318 pp.—a well-written, accessible account that articulates the "radical perspective" on Paul (as a Jew and within Judaism)

Litwa, M. David. *We Are Being Transformed: Deification in Paul's Soteriology*. Beihefte zur Zeitschrift für die neutestamentliche Wissenschaft 187. Berlin: de Gruyter, 2012—a bold, exciting account of Paul's ideas about "deification"

Wright, N. T. *Paul and the Faithfulness of God*. 2 vols. Minneapolis: Fortress, 2013—a summarizing, well-written, and quite strongly theologically oriented overall account of Paul

———. **Paul and His Recent Interpreters*. London: SPCK, 2015, 379 pp.—an excellent read for the non-expert who wishes to understand the development of Pauline scholarship as seen from Wright's theologically oriented perspective

Barclay, John M. G. *Paul and the Gift*. Grand Rapids, MI: Eerdmans, 2015—a magisterial account of a crucial concept in Paul that combines a fine-grained historical perspective with a strong theological sensitivity

Nanos, Mark D., and Magnus Zetterholm, eds. *Paul within Judaism: Restoring the First-Century Context to the Apostle*. Minneapolis: Fortress, 2015—a programmatic statement of the "radical perspective" on Paul; not always an easy read

Sampley, J. Paul, ed. *Paul in the Greco-Roman World: A Handbook*. Harrisburg, PA: Trinity, 2003; 2nd ed. Vol. 2. London: Bloomsbury, 2016—a collection of essays by an international group of experts

Thiessen, Matthew. *Paul and the Gentile Problem*. Oxford: Oxford University Press, 2016—a probing analysis by one of the foremost spokesmen for the "radical perspective" on Paul

*Fredriksen, Paula. *Paul: The Pagans' Apostle*. New Haven, CT: Yale University Press, 2017, 319 pp.—the best summarizing articulation so far of the "radical perspective" on Paul; splendidly written

CHAPTER 1

See in particular Schweitzer 1998/1931 and Fredriksen 2017. Also this:

Engberg-Pedersen, Troels. *Cosmology and Self in the Apostle Paul: The Material Spirit*. Oxford: Oxford University Press, 2010

CHAPTER 2

Engberg-Pedersen, Troels. *Paul and the Stoics*. Edinburgh: T&T Clark, 2000—not exactly an easy read

CHAPTER 3

See in particular Schweitzer 1998/1931, Munck 1959/1954, Stendahl 1976, Dahl 1977, Sanders 1977 and 1983, Räisänen 1983, Stowers 1994, Watson 2007, Eisenbaum 2009, Nanos and Zetterholm 2015, Thiessen 2016, and Fredriksen 2017. Also this:

Gager, John G. *Who Made Early Christianity? The Jewish Lives of the Apostle Paul*. New York: Columbia University Press, 2015—another important contribution to the "radical" Paul

CHAPTER 4

Harrill, J. Albert. *Slaves in the New Testament: Literary, Social, and Moral Dimensions*. Minneapolis: Fortress, 2006—a splendid discussion

———. *"Paul and Slavery." In *Paul in the Greco-Roman World*, edited by J. Paul Sampley, 301–345. Vol. 2. London: Bloomsbury, 2016—a well-written update

Kraemer, Ross S., and Mary Rose D'Angelo, eds. *Women and Christian Origins*. New York: Oxford University Press, 1999—with two summarizing essays by Margaret Y. MacDonald and Elizabeth Castelli

*Martin, Dale B. *Sex and the Single Savior: Gender and Sexuality in Biblical Interpretation*. Louisville, KY: Westminster John Knox, 2006, 268 pp.—covers most relevant topics in Paul; very well written

CHAPTERS 5–6

Starr, James, and Troels Engberg-Pedersen, eds. *Early Christian Paraenesis in Context*. Beihefte zur Zeitschrift für die neutestamentliche Wissenschaft 125. Berlin: de Gruyter, 2004—a collection of essays by an international group of experts

Vegge, Ivar. *2 Corinthians—a Letter about Reconciliation*. Wissenschaftliche Untersuchungen zum Neuen Testament 2.239. Tübingen,

Germany: Mohr Siebeck, 2008—a convincing defense of the unity of the canonical letter

CONCLUSION

*Fukuyama, Francis. *Identity: The Demand for Dignity and the Politics of Resentment.* New York: Farrar, Straus & Giroux, 2018, 218 pp.—a most valuable contribution on a hot issue in current politics (note that its subtitle is different in the British version published the same year in London by Profile Books: *Contemporary Identity Politics and the Struggle for Recognition*)

Schildkraut, Deborah. "National Identity in the United States." In *Handbook of Identity Theory and Research*, edited by Seth J. Schwartz, Koen Luyckx, and Vivian L. Vignoles, 845–865. Vol. 2. New York: Springer, 2011—a thoroughly researched empirical overview

PAUL AND PHILOSOPHY—HISTORICALLY

See in particular Engberg-Pedersen 2000 and 2010 (above, under chapters 1 and 2). Also this:

*Malherbe, Abraham J. *Paul and the Thessalonians.* Philadelphia: Fortress, 1987, 120 pp.—a splendid introduction to Malherbe's philosophical and social historical approach; crisply written

———. *Light from the Gentiles: Hellenistic Philosophy and Early Christianity.* 2 vols. Edited by Carl R. Holladay, John T. Fitzgerald, Gregory E. Sterling, and James W. Thompson. Supplements to Novum Testamentum 150/1–2. Leiden: Brill, 2014—collected works; a massive masterpiece

Wasserman, Emma. *The Death of the Soul in Romans 7: Sin, Death, and the Law in Light of Hellenistic Psychology.* Wissenschaftliche Untersuchungen zum Neuen Testament 2.256. Tübingen, Germany: Mohr Siebeck, 2008—a strong defense of the Platonic influence on Paul

Thorsteinsson, Runar M. *Roman Christianity and Roman Stoicism: A Comparative Study of Ancient Morality.* Oxford: Oxford University Press, 2010—a crisp, sharply focused analysis

Dodson, Joseph R., and David E. Briones, eds. *Paul and Seneca in Dialogue*. Leiden: Brill, 2017—a collection of essays by an international group of experts

Dodson, Joseph R., and David E. Briones, eds. *Paul and the Giants of Philosophy: Reading the Apostle in Greco-Roman Context*. Downers Grove, IL: IVP, 2019—a collection of essays by an international group of experts

PAUL AND PHILOSOPHY—IN A CONTEMPORARY CONTEXT

Taubes, Jacob. *The Political Theology of Paul*. Stanford, CA: Stanford University Press, 2004 (German 1993)—a fascinating reappropriation of Paul by a Jewish philosopher and apocalypticist

*Badiou, Alain. *Saint Paul: The Foundation of Universalism*. Stanford, CA: Stanford University Press, 2003, 111 pp. (French 1997)—the best modern analysis by a philosopher of stature; crisply written but not easy

Agamben, Giorgio. *The Time That Remains: A Commentary on the Letter to the Romans*. Stanford, CA: Stanford University Press, 2005 (Italian 2000)—a probing analysis of Paul's messianism by a contemporary political philosopher; not easy

Caputo, John D., and Linda M. Alcoff, eds. *St. Paul among the Philosophers*. Bloomington: Indiana University Press, 2009—a collection of essays by an international group of experts

Blanton, Ward, and Hent de Vries, eds. *Paul and the Philosophers*. New York: Fordham University Press, 2013—a collection of essays by an international group of experts

Frick, Peter, ed. *Paul in the Grip of the Philosophers: The Apostle and Contemporary Philosophy*. Minneapolis: Fortress, 2013—a collection of essays by an international group of experts

van der Heiden, Gert-Jan, George van Kooten, and Antonio Cimino, eds. *Saint Paul and Philosophy: The Consonance of Ancient and Modern Thought*. Berlin: de Gruyter, 2017—a collection of essays by an international group of experts

ANCIENT TEXTS